A Second Naturalists's Guide
to Lakeland Waterfalls
throughout the year

First Published March 1987

ISBN 0 902272 65 9

Printed and Published by
Westmorland Gazette, Kendal, England.

A Second Naturalist's Guide to Lakeland Waterfalls throughout the year

By Mary Welsh

Contents

Contents *(Continued)*

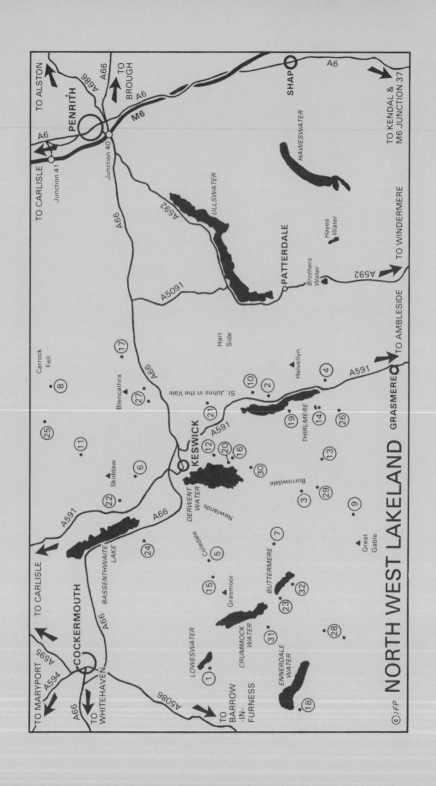

© IFP NORTH WEST LAKELAND

Foreword

This is Mary Welsh's second book on Lakeland Waterfalls and a worthy successor to the first, in which she guided her readers on walks to the waterfalls of Southern Lakeland, with notes on the fauna and flora seen along the way.

In this volume her explorations take her to North-Western Lakeland, where by following the becks to their lonely beginnings in the fells she has discovered many falls rarely seen by visitors, and tells of them and their natural surroundings quite delightfully.

A feature of the book is the artistry of her illustrator, David Macaulay.

AWainwright

Holme Force, Loweswater

Holme Force, Loweswater

Loweswater lies north of Crummock Water and Buttermere. The latter are surrounded by tall mountains that rise steeply from their shores. Loweswater sits amid more gentle surroundings, and there are farms at either end. Darling Fell and Low Fell lie to the north-east with Burnbank Fell and Blake Fell to the west. On New Year's Day they are without snow, unlike the mountains that surround the other two lakes. Holme Beck rises high on the slopes of Burnbank Fell and tumbles through Holme Wood in a series of lovely falls on its way to the lake. To reach these falls, park by the telephone box on the lake side of the road between the Grange Hotel and Loweswater Hall. Take the signposted footpath by the lay-by and cross two fields and two stiles to a metalled road leading to Hudson Place. Ash and hawthorn compose the hedge and, below, the bracken is still very green. The hawthorn, laden with berries, have attracted several fieldfare which are enjoying the abundance. They fly off, calling harshly as they go, showing their dark brown tails and wings and grey-buff rumps.

Beyond Hudson Place there is a lovely berried holly by the gate that gives access to a lane leading towards the wood. Here a pair of robin consort aggressively. The lane is deep in fallen oak leaves. Foxglove and bramble are a rich green and in a field beyond the walk is a spindly lamb, the first

Pochard

of the year. The lane ends in a gate and a path leads on close to the water. It is shallow here and iced over. Beyond the ice a pack of mallard swim idly on the still water, together with dozens of bobbing coot. Among all these ducks swims one pochard. Its head is a rich chestnut and its upper parts grey, fine pencilled with black lines. On the other side of the path the fell is clothed in a brown mantle of dead bracken and patches of grass.

Enter the wood by throughs in a drystone wall and follow the path beneath densely shading fir trees. The path passes splendid mature oaks which, now leafless, give views of the lake beyond. When a clump of Scots pine is reached, take a path that turns right and then bears left. This brings the walker near to Holme Force, the object of the walk. The water falling through the gill is all that can now be heard.

There is an excellent view of the Force from the path. It tumbles over a tiny precipice high in a larch plantation and drops in several long white falls. Then racing water slides down a rocky slipway. It hits a low wall of rock across its pathway so fiercely that the water spouts into the air and then falls in a long arc, leaving trails of glistening drops as it goes. The beck falls to the right into a pool, then divides into several streams before reaching another

From here
it hurtles in one long white jet
into a hollow by the path.

pool. From here it hurtles in one long, white jet into a hollow by the path, where is races around huge boulders and passes under the small drystone bridge which carries the path.

Oak and ash shadow the gill and its rocky sides are clad in grass, bracken, wood sorrel, moss and reed. Icicles and sheets of ice have formed along the edges of the roaring water and one large icicle stands sentinel-like at the bottom of the last fall. To see the full beauty of the Force climb the left side of the fall. There is an indistinct path and part of the way requires

3

scrambling over large boulders. The close view of the waterfall is very rewarding.

Eventually a fence bordering the wood bars the way but across the fence the beck is seen tumbling, hurrying, gurgling through the larch-lined gill that cuts through the open fell. Look to your right at the exposed rock faces on either side of the beck. Oak roots creep into almost every crevice of the layers upon layers of Skiddaw slate. Follow the fence along the edge of the wood. Here two woodcock crouching low feed quietly under the dense conifers, a carpet of brown needles providing the

Path through Holme Wood.

perfect camouflage. When disturbed these warm-brown, plump-breasted birds take off and fly low, zig-zagging through the trees.

Two hundred yards or so along the fence a good path, sloping downwards and eastwards, falls away to the left. Descend this, crossing three forest rides that traverse Holme Wood, until the shore is reached. It is exhilarating to come down such a long way after the climb to the Force.

By the lake, a dipper flies close to the water, rotund and short-tailed and calling "zit, zit, zit" as it goes. It settles on a small fence at the water's edge, then flies to the shore and runs into the water, causing a

A dipper runs into the water.

considerable wake. It surfaces regularly, returning to the shore again. Then with its short wings whirring rapidly it crosses to the other side of the lake. To the right from this end of the lake is the great cleft of Gasgale Gill with Grasmoor, its guardian, above. To the left on the other shore is Loweswater Hall, sombrely Victorian among its trees.

Walk back along the shore path through stately beech and massive oak. A log footbridge crosses Holme Beck as it races to the lake. Very soon the walker reaches the clump of pine and the path to the Force. The circle of Holme Wood is complete.

O.S. Map NY118217
2½ miles

Waterfalls in Helvellyn Gill, Thirlmere

The charming waterfalls in Helvellyn Gill lie below the towering Lower Man. The latter is a peak where several paths meet and then lead to Helvellyn itself. On a bright January day when snow has fallen overnight, the walk to the falls is through an enchanted world.

The gated path leaves the car park on the A591 opposite the Station Coppice car park and leads to a wooden bridge over the chattering beck. The track comes to a stile in a drystone wall and gives access to the corner of a conifer plantation. This is transformed into a fairy forest, each needle carrying a delicate dusting of snow. The few deciduous trees among the fir are dressed entirely in white, revealing every branch.

A fairy forest

7

The path rises above the trees and the fell towers upwards.
Here the bracken is buried in snow and those fronds that do rear
above it are bent double and quite dead. A carrion crow uses its
powerful beak to clear snow from a large patch of ground by
flicking it to one side and then the other so that it can probe into
the sheltered soil below. After several stabs it lifts its beak and
moves to a boulder to enjoy the large trophy it has found. It is
approached submissively by another and the second bird is offered
a morsel. Then this visitor to the feast is moved away by a
sideways shove, the first crow returning to its food-seeking in the
prepared patch.

A black-headed gull, now in its winter plumage, with its head
bearing only a spot of black, circles overhead, its legs and beak
dark red. It leaves the snow-covered fell for the more hospitable
waters of Thirlmere. A common gull, with its greenish yellow bill
and legs, careens above and then it too returns to the lake.

Several small streams are crossed and the main beck is
recrossed by a large wooden bridge. From here the tumbling

Lower Fall

waterfalls can be seen. They drop in a long series of small falls, the water grey against the sparkling snow. Gone are the foaming cascades that usually delight the eye. Now the waters that would swell the beck so that it would race in fury are frozen in the ground and it will be some time before the wintry weather releases its grip.

The birch and ash that line the gill are heavy with snow and each tiny alder catkin bears its load. The trunks of the trees steam in the cold air of the gill as they receive the heat of the sun. A flock of young male chaffinch fly into the trees and then they are gone, their breasts, as yet a soft pink, bright against the blue sky.

The path continues beside the beck for a little way and from here there is a good view of the waterfalls, but the snow muffles

the sound of the falling water. Rejoin the main path which leads on, up over the crisp snow, towards the shining peak above, where a small snowstorm is stirred by the icy winds blowing high above.

Young male chaffinches

O.S. Map NY322167
1½ miles

Scaleclose Force, Borrowdale

Sometimes late in January, after days and days of rain, the sun comes out and bathes the Lake District in a translucent light. Long, thin shadows are thrown by leafless trees, distant mountains appear close at hand and snow-topped peaks sparkle and are a brilliant white against the blue sky. If all this beauty is accompanied by a gentle mildness then a walk to a waterfall is a delight. To visit Scaleclose Force, park at Seatoller Barn, a National Trust car park provided with toilets. Here birch and young conifer are alive with chaffinch, great tit, blue tit and robin all in full song and nuptial plumage. Spring seems close at hand.

Take the path that leads to a gate at the north-eastern corner. Beyond is a wide grassy path that crosses a small beck leading to another gate. Fine oak, widely spaced, give the air of well planned parkland. Continue on through another gate along a wide, stony track to a gate into Johnny Wood. A kestrel sits very still in an oak, watching for any movement below and enjoying the unusual warmth of the sun. When a wide gap is reached in an old wall, where a gate might once have been, turn left and follow a track that swings uphill through ancient oaks and some young ones, newly planted. Here a nuthatch gives its loud boy-like whistle and then is seen scurrying down the branches, probing crevices as it goes. It flies to another oak and this time climbs upwards and then is joined by another. Both are blue-grey above and rich chestnut below, with a conspicuous black eye-streak. Scattered among the oak are several holly and these have attracted a horde of mistle-thrush and blackbird which are devouring the few remaining berries.

The track zig-zags until the fell wall is reached. Then it becomes rock-strewn and moves into the trees, leaving the wall away to the left. Deeper into the wood the colour imperceptibly changes from the russet of the deep carpet of oak leaves to a rich velvet green where every rock and tree trunk is clothed in moss. Continue on the indistinct track, following a very narrow trod as it winds steeply up the craggy slope. Rejoin the fell wall and look for a ladder stile on to the open fell below High Doat. Turn right and follow a sheep trod close by the wall and then beside a fence. The latter protects the walker and sheep from the sheer downward sloping crag.

The trod climbs steadily and there are wonderful views, with the Jaws of Borrowdale ahead and Derwentwater and Blencathra in the distance. Below to the right lies Johnny Wood, where birch and larch mingle with the ancient oak. Trees cover the exceedingly steep slope almost to the edge of the River Derwent, the village of Rosthwaite lying snugly in the valley bottom on the far side of the hurrying, beautifully blue beck.

As the path climbs, the snow-topped peaks around Buttermere and Crummock Water come into view. In time, a stile is reached and from here the noise of the beck can be heard filling the air.

A good path leads down the steep fellside, crossing a damp valley bottom, only to rise again to a ladder stile over the fell wall. Turn right and cross a wooden bridge over the beck, continuing along a wide track until the fell wall is breached by a gate. Walk straight ahead from the gate to the beck. Here purple-topped moss thrusts upwards in the grip of hard frost. The frozen ground makes it a tedious climb down to the edge of the gill but the sound of the Force draws one on. Even from the gill edge the Force remains hidden and the walker must clamber down to the side of the water. A few steps upstream and the lovely

Moss

Force lies ahead. It tumbles headlong over a precipice in an elegant fall of white tresses into a blue pool surrounded by a C-shaped rim of boulders. These boulders, the sloping sides of the gill and all the trunks of trees are blanketed thickly with various species of moss.

Honeysuckle already in leaf clasps boulders and branches alike and a trailing tendril with a long, thin icicle adhering to its swings over the plummeting water. Bracken and polypody flourish where they can. Enchanter's nightshade still retains bright green leaves and celandine, wood sorrel and golden saxifrage push their way through the enveloping moss. Bilberry, not yet in leaf, thrives and liverwort covers every wet perpendicular surface behind and beside the curtain of water that descends into the secluded hollow.

Golden Saxifrage

To return, follow the beck to a small wooden bridge and then walk along a path to the edge of Johnny Wood. Here, lovely old oak trees flank the path. Occasionally pigeons blunder through the higher branches as they

Honeysuckle

are disturbed but otherwise Johnny Wood

13

is all one's own — a gloriously quiet, soft seclusion. Above to the right the slopes are steep and long icicles hang from jagged outcrops. The warm sun has melted the outer layers of ice and in the silvan stillness the drips can be heard falling on the ice-covered boulders below.

Pass Longthwaite and its graceful bridge over the Derwent. Continue on the same side of the river past the youth hostel and then along a rather indistinct path among the rocks bordering the gently flowing water. A good path passes between a wire fence and a steep rock face to the edge of Johnny Wood, where jays call raucously and a buzzard wings slowly from one oak to another. After several gates the first path of the walk is regained and here tree creeper hurry up the huge trunks and blue tit call and disport in the warm sun.

Bridge over Derwent – Longthwaite

O.S. Map NY246147
3½ miles

Waterfalls in Birkside Gill, Thirlmere

Waterfalls in Birkside Gill, Thirlmere

The silvery beck that flows through Birkside Gill gathers water from the slopes of Dollywagon Pike. It tumbles over a precipice in a wide fan of white water, then, where an ash hangs over the beck, it hurries on to fall in a foaming jet. It passes more ash trees, dropping in another long, foam-topped stream of water. Rocky projections part the water and several small falls occur before a large pinnacle of rock causes the beck to rage downwards in two more fan-like drops. The beck divides once more and two chattering streams noisily flow over their rocky beds.

Wythburn Church.

One tributary comes close to a solitary Scots pine. The other passes through a shallow, narrow cleft, tangling momentarily with the roots of an alder, and then both flow under wooden bridges — soon to join again. United, the beck races on to enter the waters of Thirlmere at Wythburn.

Wythburn Church is on the A591. A good place to start the walk to these lovely waterfalls is from the car park behind the church, where a gate at the entrance leads to a path through the forest. Each part of the forest has a different coniferous species —

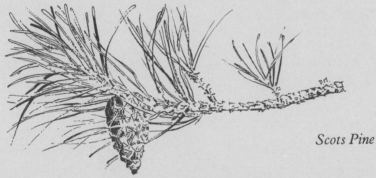

Scots Pine

sometimes cypress or fir or pine or larch. The path is too close to the road for real peace but gives the walker good views of the lake. Sturdy wooden bridges enable the walker to cross dry-shod the small becks that flow down to the lake.

The forest ends and the spectacular waterfalls lie ahead and above. Early in the New Year the water sparkles in the sunlight and the blue sky is reflected in the pools, but to the right, on Willie Wife Moor, spring seems a long way off. The fell, covered with withered grass and lichen-encrusted rocks, is fast in the grip of winter.

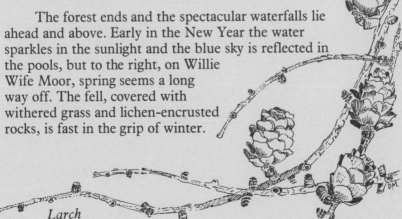

Larch

The forest ride makes a u-turn and passes back through the coniferous trees but higher up the fell and well away from the road. Here goldcrest and chaffinch haunt the trees. Overhead can be heard the screaming calls of a pair of peregrine falcon and then they pass high above the ride — black arcs against the blue sky. Suddenly one swoops downwards after its prey and is lost to sight.

The forest ride is covered with needles that are soft to walk on. They muffle footsteps and this allows the walker to hear not only the birds but also the foxhounds that are out on the slopes of Helvellyn.

Lichen encrusted rock.

Where the ride is gated for a second time a signpost points the way down to the Wythburn car park.

O.S. Map NY328125
2 miles

Low Force and High Force, Coledale

Low Force and High Force, Coledale

The village of Braithwaite lies west of Keswick and is reached by the A66 and the B5292. Look for a small parking area on the left just beyond the village at the start of the Whinlatter Pass. This is where the mine road to Low Force begins. Pass through the gate and walk the two miles to the foot of this great fall of water.

The road lies high on the fellside above the snaking Coledale Beck, now covered with white ice. It makes its way through banks of birch whose young branches are flushed with a gentle red. To the right the fell rises steeply for 150 feet or more. Broken and bent bracken stalks protrude through the snow and the few flowers on the gorse add a touch of gold in the surprisingly warm February sun.

Pass through another gate and ahead lies the road, continuing on and on to the foot of a towering wedge of rock — Force Crag. To the right is Long Crag and a snow-covered Grisedale Pike rising above. To the left and ahead is Bell Crag. Overtopping all others, and carrying a deep burden of snow, is Grasmoor.

Gorse.

The valley seems deserted at first but soon the walker comes upon some hardy sheep. A robin stays hidden in a gorse bush and then, when trouble has passed, it returns to hunting through the roadside vegetation. A pair of meadow pipit, overwintering on the fells, run across the verge where the snow has gone, their movements jerky and their outer tail feathers as white as snow; as yet there are no nuptial flights or signs of spring plumage but they keep close together as if they have already paired, and flit ahead for a long way along the road. Overhead passes a raven. It slides down through the clear sky in a magnificent arc and is lost to sight over Crag Hill.

A cloud passes across the sky and sunlight races along the fellside, picking out the greens and browns where the snow has slipped. From one of these patches several fieldfare rise, calling harshly as they go, their grey heads and rumps identifying them as they fly low just ahead of the walker.

And then the New Coledale Mine is reached. This was opened two years ago by a partnership seeking the barytes and zinc hidden in the depths of the mountain. Smoke rises from the generator shed and yellow-helmeted miners scurry over the slopes. Railway tracks run into the heart of the mountain. Spoil heaps tower overhead, amazingly dwarfed by the great wall of rock that blocks the valley, Force Crag. The mine scars and defaces the valley head but buildings, heaps and shafts are softened today by a blanket of snow, and the hillside that is deeply tunnelled by man's efforts to wrest barytes from its inner recesses remains austere, aloof and outwardly intact.

Railway tracks run into the heart of the mountain.

Beyond is the inaptly named Pudding Beck which usually leaps over Force Crag to join the Coledale far below. Today the excitement of the beck has been caught and held in ice.

Great icicles hang for many feet, catching the wintry sun. Several intrepid youngsters climb the frozen fall on ropes attached to the topmost part of this icy cataract.

A wide track on the left leaves the mine road just before the buildings. Cross the Coledale by large square stepping stones and then follow the path as it swings upwards, keeping to the left of Force Crag.

The track is reinforced by broken rock and at some time in the past has been drained by huge iron pipes, now red with rust. In spite of these, much water must have washed over the path and been frozen in the bitter cold, turning it into a sheet of ice that must now be negotiated with care.

Path to High Force, Coledale.

Follow the track as it bears away to the right and into a natural amphitheatre crossed by Pudding Beck just before it drops over Force Crag. Ahead is High Force, a twin to Low Force. Pudding Beck here too has its impetuosity frozen into a myriad of icicles. Derelict mine buildings lie to the right, high up, cloaked in snow, with black, gaping holes where windows and shutters once kept out the fearsome weather. This is an isolated, desolate place in the winter but in spring life returns and the meadow pipit rear their young and wheatear flit from rock to rock. Saxifrage flowers in the beck and the earth is covered with tormentil, bright among the heather.

O.S. Map NY196215   NY192215
6 miles

22

*Waterfall on Slades Beck,
Millbeck, Skiddaw.*

Waterfall on Slades Beck, Millbeck, Skiddaw.

S ometimes in late February Skiddaw and its Little Man are bathed in sunlight all day long. The high slopes are covered in deep snow and the tops of these two ancient mountains rear up, white peaked, into a deep blue sky. Occasionally a biting north wind picks up the dry snow and swirls it round and round in miniature whirls that spiral down the smooth slopes with no crags or precipices to hinder their progress.

Below lies the village of Millbeck, basking in the sunshine and sheltered from the wind that is racing across the tops. Here the walk to the waterfall begins.

Leave Keswick by the north-bound A591. A mile and a quarter from the roundabout on the A66 turn right at the signpost for the village. At the first junction turn left and park on the immediate right.

Cross the bridge over the beck, pass Millbeck Farm and continue along the lane for 100 yards. Turn right, following the signpost direction for Skiddaw. Pass through the wooden kissing- gate to a path where ivy, bramble and laurel leaves show bright green against dead bracken dusted with snow.

After passing through a second kissing-gate,

Follow a wide snowy track.

follow a wide snowy track that inclines slightly to the right. Ahead stand the mountains. To the right lies a small plantation of larch, each tree bending slightly where it has submitted over the years to strong winds from the west. Long dark shadows are thrown across the undisturbed white floor of the wood.

Fieldfare on immediate slopes.

To the left the immediate slopes have lost much of their snow and a large flock of fieldfare feed among the grass where the ground is softened after the long hours of warm sun. The birds move from one green patch to another, the white of their bellies and underwings very noticeable as they catch the sun in flight. Twenty or more birds are busy feeding on worms and insects that have also responded to the warmth. The path passes close to some lofty cypress, heavy with tiny opened cones. Magpies court and chatter and coal tit fill the air with their incessant, strident calls.

Pass through the gate, turning right and keeping close to the edge of the wood along a track, wide and snow-bound. A pair of meadow pipit, keeping close together, flit across the fell, occasionally settling on an outcrop of rock.

The tiny, opened cone of some lofty cypress.

Step across the little beck that cuts the path and pause awhile, noticing the contrasting environs through which it passes on its way to join with Slades Beck. Above, it flows through a desolate, barren gill. Below, it tumbles into the wood and is cradled by spruce and cypress through which passes enough light for bracken and moss to flourish.

The path continues to the edge of Slades Beck and its small dams. These are in disrepair. A stride enables the walker to reach the other side of the beck and then follow a path that keeps close to the dancing water. Glistening icicles have formed wherever water has seeped off the fell to join the exuberant beck.

Small falls drop through snowy banks where crowd rowan, larch and a sturdy sycamore whose buds are fat and green. The path struggles on between broken, lichened rocks, they too having shed their mantle of snow in the afternoon sun. The path is a sheet of ice where a cascade of water has washed across. It passes under a tall, solitary larch, the long exposed roots of which clasp the rock. Cutting through the snowy fellside are bright green flushes where small becks flow and a profusion of tiny plants cover the ground.

The path passes under a tall, solitary larch.

The path has been restored in places and leads to a railed area and another dam, this one small but deep and in good condition. At this point, climb up the fellside to a narrow sheep track. From here the waterfall, which is really a series of tiny falls, drops in a flurry of white water. It is fast-flowing and boisterous and with a delicate charm of its own.

On the opposite bank, beneath several rowan that grow against a steepish rockface, are two sturdy Herdwick nibbling at grass growing among polypody, heather and ivy. They have found a sunny haven, free of snow and out of the wind. Above them the steep slopes of Little Man and Skiddaw are momentarily blurred as a snow storm moves across the tops.

On the way back, enjoy the wonderful panorama. The Vale of Keswick lies below, with its lake frozen. Beyond are the mountains of the north-west lakes, with the peaks of Grasmoor, Robinson and Grisedale Pike covered with snow. Close at hand the sun bleaches the green from the trees and the flushes but turns the beck to pure gold, the only colour now to be seen.

Woodland litter

O.S. Map NY261268
2 miles

28

Waterfall on Scope Beck, Little Dale, Newlands.

Chapel Bridge.

Leave the A66 at the turn-off for Braithwaite. Turn left in the village, taking the narrow road signposted for Buttermere. This runs beneath the broad flank of Barrow. Below, to the left, Newlands Beck flows through gentle pastures where sheep graze and the sun throws long shadows across the grass. Continue along the road where it skirts Causey Pike, turning left at the sign for Little Town. Cross Keskadale Beck by a small, picturesque, drystone bridge. Follow the narrow lane for another hundred yards and carefully negotiate the very narrow Chapel Bridge, another beautiful construction in stone, built many years ago. Just beyond is space for several cars.

Newlands Church.

29

After putting on walking boots, recross the bridge and take an even narrower gated lane that leads to Newlands Church, a pretty white building set among oak and pollarded ash, with the Keskadale flowing merrily beyond.

Tall oak and slender birch line the lane as it begins to climb towards Low High Snab, now cottages. Soon these are replaced by thorn through which a mixed flock of tit move noisily and agilely. A robin sings plaintively, undisturbed by intruders passing through its territory.

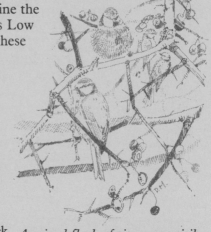

Two gates on either side of the cottages keep the garden free from the attentions of sheep and here snowdrops grow and honeysuckle is covered with reddish leaves. The metalled track ends and a rough path continues to another gate. This gives access

A mixed flock of tit move noisily and agilely through thorn.

to the open fell and a first good view of the Scope sparkling in the valley bottom as it winds its way through silver birch, with young twigs glowing a rich red in the bright sunlight.

Keep to the path as it moves on to the fell, which is now sparsely covered with scrubby gorse. Before long the bushes become more dense and some have pale yellow buds. Walking is sheer joy as the path widens and the turf springs against the boot. The track then begins to climb and the beck tumbles in white foam along its rocky bed, catching the sun as it races around impeding boulders. Beneath a solitary rowan is a small fall and close to the water's edge a crow preens in the sunshine. Flushes of green run down the slopes to the beck below. Continual run off has encouraged a rich growth of sphagnum and common hair moss.

Eventually a barrier across the valley, seen for some time, is reached. It is an old dam made of large even-sized rocks covered with moss and bleached grass and it holds back an ancient reservoir that is now a charming pool. To one side of the dam is a narrow breach through which cascades the beck, white-topped as it drops over a steep, ridged rock-face. Here grows another rowan.

At mid-day in mid-March the sun comes over the top of Hindscarth and illuminates the little valley. It also highlights the dramatic cleft in the skyline above, through which the Scope Beck leaves Little Dale and leaps impetuously into its steep-sided gorge. The water races downwards, angrily negotiating huge projections that would thwart its passage. It hurtles down a rocky slip-way and then drops again in another long curtain of white. A searching wind races through the cleft above and picks up the water of the beck and funnels it up into the air, tossing the spray wantonly this way and that. It is a delightful waterfall, dropping a long way into this secluded, isolated valley. The only evidence of human life is the momentary glimpses of matchstick figures hurrying along the ridges to the tops. The slopes above the gorge are littered with huge boulders and rich red-brown clay oozes from beneath. On the opposite side is the sheer face of High Crags, a patchwork of bright green algae, rust-red bracken and rush and grey rock. Pause here and enjoy the view back along the valley to the distant Skiddaw and Blencathra, still with snow in their gullies and over-shadowing Derwentwater.

Then a drama takes place on the perpendicular side of High Crags above the waterfall. A peregrine flies to the face and sits almost motionless on a nest of twigs on a rock ledge. It has a slate-coloured back and head

A Peregrine sits motionless on a nest of twigs.

31

and a barred breast with white under its bright yellow beak. It stays a long time, moving only its head. Then out of the sky hurtles a furious raven, the owner of the twiggy nest. It sends the peregrine on its way. The raven croaks "pruk, pruk, pruk" several times and then, perhaps not quite ready to use the old nest itself, flies upwards, to enjoy the crosswinds high above.

Rowan in winter

O.S. Map NY214177
4 miles

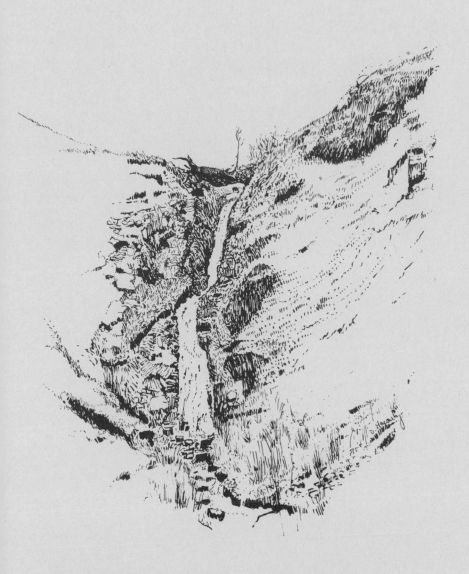

Waterfall in Brandy Gill,
Carrock Fell

*Ring Ousel
and
grass seedhead*

Waterfall in Brandy Gill, Carrock Fell

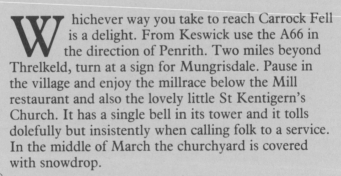

Whichever way you take to reach Carrock Fell is a delight. From Keswick use the A66 in the direction of Penrith. Two miles beyond Threlkeld, turn at a sign for Mungrisdale. Pause in the village and enjoy the millrace below the Mill restaurant and also the lovely little St Kentigern's Church. It has a single bell in its tower and it tolls dolefully but insistently when calling folk to a service. In the middle of March the churchyard is covered with snowdrop.

Beyond Mungrisdale is the hamlet of Mosedale, and a left turn between the River Caldew and the telephone box is signposted Swineside. The mine road leading to the waterfall starts here. If approaching from Carlisle, spend some time in Caldbeck and visit another church dedicated to St Kentigern. This one is large and has been much restored since it was built in Norman times. John Peel is buried in the churchyard.

Continue on to Hesket Newmarket, with its old houses built around a green. Follow the signs for Mungrisdale. Just before Mosedale, look for the steep slopes of Carrock Fell, formed of gabbro, a hard igneous rock. Take the mine road that leaves on the right beyond the telephone box. The road has a metalled surface and skirts the boulder-strewn Caldew. The water hurries on its way north, surging white-topped around huge rocks, some of Skiddaw granite, a soft pink in the strengthening sun.

Drive along the road slowly, enjoying the pastures and their sheep, the juniper-clad slopes, the beck and the steep sides of Bowscale Fell. Better still, walk the two miles to the end of the tarmaced road. At the end of the road is a solidly-built bridge over Grainsgill Beck. Beyond, a wide track leads to Skiddaw House and then on to Whitewater Dash, a waterfall yet to be visited. To the left, just over the bridge, is a side track where a car can be parked.

Recross the bridge and follow another track that passes the derelict, galvanised-iron buildings of a mine once used for obtaining wolfram. Railway lines lead into the belly of the mountain. The entrance is closed with a metal door but a wide stream of water flows from beneath it to swell the water of Grainsgill Beck before it unites with the Caldew.

Immediately beyond the mine buildings a single track turns right by the side of the beck that tumbles through Brandy Gill. Keep to the track that climbs the fellside and is at a safe distance from mine workings and open shafts. Look back to Coombe Height,

Old mine buildings

towering over the side valleys of the Caldew. Its top is streaked with snow and its slopes are criss-crossed with straight lines — mining levels ending in spoil heaps. Lower is a stone, turret-topped entrance to an old mine and below is a huge heap of shattered quartz.

Continue along narrow trods into the gill. Frequent rock falls and landslips make it necessary for the walker to cross the little beck several times, but generally a step suffices, or there are strategically placed rocks. Moss is growing well now that spring is on its way and is a bright green among the bleached grass. Every slope is littered with boulders, making Carrock Fell quite different from the grassy giants nearby. The trods climb further into the gill, where the woody stems of heather are festooned with various species of lichen. Then, hidden in a fold of the land, lies the foaming waterfall — a white delight. Across the top the ancient rowan, featured in Wainwright's guide to the northern fells, has since fallen, its roots succumbing to the constant shifting of soil and scree. It lies across the rocky shelf over which the little beck tumbles, boisterously, in a flurry of foam. At first the water cascades and then descends in a long frothing jet. White quartz sparkles behind the tracery of water and side rocks are covered with algae, moss, liverwort and saxifrage. The water drops into a wide, clear pool and then flows merrily on its way. This is a verdant, sheltered corner set among nature at its most severe, desolate and wild. Above the fall are more rowan and the first view of High Pike,
with a scattering of snow in its gullies. The little beck is still bordered with trods, sometimes on one side and then the other. Again in a secluded fold is another fall, a small, charming flurry of water, beside it a dark, damp cave hollowed out of solid rock.

*Another small fall close
to a dark, damp cave.*

O.S. Map NY324335
3 miles

36

*Taylorgill Force, Seathwaite,
Borrowdale*

Taylorgill Force, Seathwaite, Borrowdale

T he walk to this spectacular waterfall starts at the hamlet of Seathwaite, in Borrowdale. Cars may be parked on the grassy verge just before the hamlet. The road ends among a tiny cluster of farm buildings and cottages.

Leave the road by an archway in the farm buildings on the right. Continue to a bridge over the Derwent. On the far side of the beck, turn left and walk past a plantation of beech and larch, where willow warbler sing in late April. Continue along the path as it begins to climb, leaving the plantation behind. Whitethroat chatter harshly in the holly scattered over the open fell. Here hawthorn and ash, with buds tightly closed, struggle to survive, and from these more whitethroat sing.

Whitethroat in holly.

The path on the west side of the Derwent continues beside the beck that tumbles through Styhead Gill. Tortoiseshell butterflies flutter ahead. The path is indistinct and involves climbing over rocks and crossing scree. Above tower the crags of Base Brown. It is an exhilarating scramble and the walker is encouraged by the wonderful views ahead of white-topped water hurtling downwards. Boulders project through the foam causing spray to be tossed high into the air. This magnificent cascade descends for 140 feet in long white tresses, against a dramatic backdrop of larch, birch and Scots pine. It fills the gill with noise.

At the top of the fall is a small grassy glade, shaded by more larch and a solitary yew. Goldcrest call "si" as they hunt among the larch roses for insects. From this quiet, secluded hollow Rosthwaite village is seen far below and High Seat and Blencathra lie huge and clear beyond the nearer fells.

After a picnic and a siesta, cross the beck and continue along the path through the gill. Much of the path has been reinforced because of the serious erosion that has taken place. This work has been sympathetically done in natural rock but one's booted feet miss the springy turf that has been lost for ever. The beck ambles peacefully here, with little suggestion of the dramatic cataract below. Wheatear, now thoroughly settled in their territories and with a clutch of eggs to look after, keep just ahead of the walker.

Once the walker is over the next brow, the beck is seen racing down a rocky slipway in a boiling mass of white water. Then it flows over rocky ledges, past boulders with sides worn smooth by continual friction. Over this show of impetuosity leans an oak, it too with buds tightly closed.

Now the way is over natural boulders, and these are tiresome to the walker, but the striking views of Great Gable, Green Gable and Great End entice one on to find the tiny tarn that lies at their feet.

Cross a wooden bridge that spans the again-cascading beck. This leads to a path that

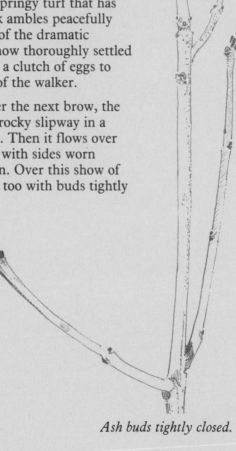

Ash buds tightly closed.

avoids a very wet area. Follow the path until the shore of Styhead Tarn is reached. Its waters are very clear and the pebbles lining the bed are multicoloured. A pair of raven fly overhead but little else disturbs the tranquillity of this isolated sheet of water surrounded by snow-topped mountains.

On the return journey retrace the path to the Force and then continue along the reinforced path, remaining on the south side of the beck. The waterfall is hidden from view by the tree-clad steep sides of the cleft but the noise of the raging water is a constant reminder of its presence. The path slopes steeply downwards beside a newly-built wall composed of many coloured rock. Pass through a stile to climb down another very steep stretch of the path that leads to the lovely drystone Stockley Bridge. Turn left over the bridge and follow the youthful Derwent, past its confluence with the water from the Force, until Seathwaite is reached once more. Here simple refreshments can be obtained.

Stockley Bridge

O.S. Map NY229109
5 miles

Waterfalls on Fisher Gill,
Thirlmere

Waterfalls on Fisher Gill, Thirlmere

When the office, the housework or even the family seem too much and you feel you must find tranquillity, the place to go is Fisher Gill. This is a long, narrow fissure on the lower slopes of White Side, part of the Helvellyn range. The walk to the gill is not arduous and it is only a short distance from the A591.

The beck tumbles over the topmost edge of the gill, divided in its fall by a huge rock, spiking upwards. Several smaller projections divide the water again so that it plunges down a long way in a wide curtain of white foam. Just before the bottom, the water drops on to a ledge that slopes to the south. It slips over this ridge, divided once again by rocky protrusions in a replica of the beauty above. It slides into a hollow surrounded by grass and heather-covered slopes. Sit here and forget the hurly-burly of modern life, watching this graceful fall of water, often blown in a fine spray by the searching wind.

In late April, even though Keswick to the north might be having its last snowfall of the winter, the steep north face of Fisher Gill shields the walker from the worst of the weather. It also protects the graceful silver birch that is covered in tiny leaves and guards the top of the fall.

Second fall

The beck hurries on over its shallow bed until it is channelled into a slip-stream between the bellying sides of the gill. Then it dawdles through another hollow, lovingly caressing the juniper-clad banks, where bilberry, foxglove and fern thrive. Here is another quiet place to meditate. Watch the peregrine glide high overhead after several rapid wing-beats.

Once more the beck is forced between a narrow gap in the gill and then topples downwards in a long, foam-covered jet. As it falls into a green-blue pool it passes holly, heather and three rowan trees, these now with delicate green leaves and flowers that are just about to open.

From now on, the water races downwards through the gill in a series of delightful small falls. It hurries past ash trees loaded with bumpy black flower buds, past honeysuckle that is a mass of blue-green leaves and willow burgeoning with life. Silver birch, covered with tiny catkins and leaves, lean over the water.

Delicate green leaves and flowers in bud.

In the larch plantation even lower down the trees are dressed in new needles and pink "roses". Eventually the beck joins St John's Beck.

To reach Fisher Gill, park in the car park at the edge of Highpark Wood. Take the wooden bridge over the beck and follow the footpath through the corner of the wood. Once over the stile, bear left, following a grassy path that rapidly joins a recently made,

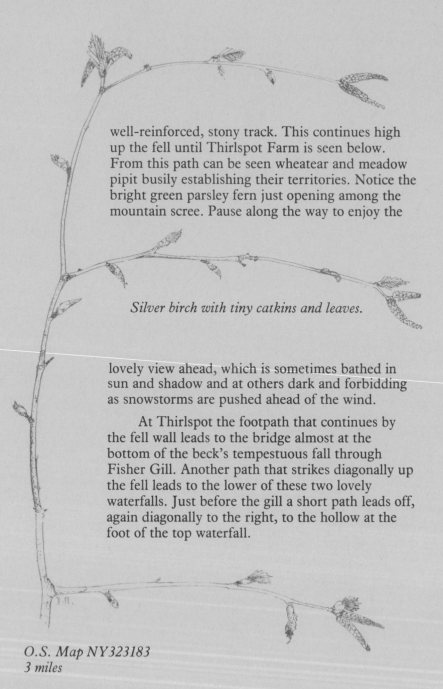

well-reinforced, stony track. This continues high up the fell until Thirlspot Farm is seen below. From this path can be seen wheatear and meadow pipit busily establishing their territories. Notice the bright green parsley fern just opening among the mountain scree. Pause along the way to enjoy the

Silver birch with tiny catkins and leaves.

lovely view ahead, which is sometimes bathed in sun and shadow and at others dark and forbidding as snowstorms are pushed ahead of the wind.

At Thirlspot the footpath that continues by the fell wall leads to the bridge almost at the bottom of the beck's tempestuous fall through Fisher Gill. Another path that strikes diagonally up the fell leads to the lower of these two lovely waterfalls. Just before the gill a short path leads off, again diagonally to the right, to the hollow at the foot of the top waterfall.

O.S. Map NY323183
3 miles

Whitewater Dash, Skiddaw

Whitewater Dash, Skiddaw

Blackthorn

I n early May, the blackthorn bushes
along the side of the A591 from
Bothel and Carlisle towards
Keswick are dressed in white blossom.
Just after Bassenthwaite, a left turn, signposted Orthwaite, leads to the Whitewater
Dash waterfall. The road is narrow and its banks
are covered with primrose, celandine and wood
sorrel. Willow warbler sing in the hawthorn
trees, now arrayed in small, pale green leaves. A
metalled farm track runs off at a right-angle to
the road at Peter House Farm. By the gated
entrance is a sign to the waterfall. In the pond
close by, water crowfoot blooms. A row of fine
Scots pine shelters the farm and the road.

The farm track has gates across it at half-
mile intervals. On either side are
wide, flat pastures supporting
numerous sheep, each with its
frisky, sturdy twin lambs. The air
resounds with the lambs' bleating
and the maternal answers. From
distant trees near Dash Farm comes
the evocative call of a cuckoo.
These are the only sounds in this
peaceful valley of the Dash; the
noise of Bank Holiday traffic and
crowds in busy Carlisle or Keswick
seems many, many miles away.

*Willow warbler
sing in
Hawthorn*

46

A row of fine Scots pine shelters the farm and the road.

Where the spectacular waterfall first comes into sight a stony track leads off to the right, running below the forbidding Dead Crags. Ahead, wheatear court and fan their tails, showing off their white feathers and meadow pipit flit from rock to boulder, keeping just beyond the walker. High up on the crags, young raven plead for food and the deep croak of the attentive parents can be heard clearly.

When immediately below the Crags, take a narrow sheep track down to the base of the waterfall. The Dash Beck is narrow and rarely deep with grassy slopes on the other side which are very inviting, so cross the water, avoiding the slippery green boulders, and eat your lunch in a hollow by the pool that receives the tumbling water. From here the view upward is very impressive. The water foams through a narrow channel and then divides into three falls that are deflected first to the left and then to the right. It falls in a wide curtain of water over spray-blackened rocks for many feet, to be finally deflected by a ridge just before it reaches the pool.

The sides of the narrow gill are lined with birch and rowan and in a holly is a twiggy nest. It is also the haunt of a solitary robin that sings its plaintive song.

Only half of this lovely fall can be seen from below. To view the remainder, recross the beck and clamber up through the heather to the path — making a mental note to return in late August when the sound of nectar-drunk bees must be profound.

The path ascends to the top of the fall, keeping close to the steep edges of the gill, giving tantalising views of the falling water. From the stile at the head of the gill the path continues on over Skiddaw Forest — a forest without a tree. Here the Dash is once more a quiet beck flowing under a tiny drystone bridge, giving few hints of its exuberant leap into the valley below.

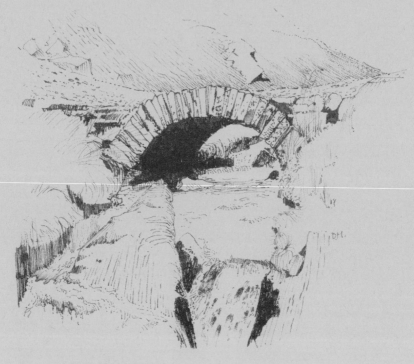

Here the Dash flows under
a tiny drystone bridge.

O.S. Map NY272314
4 miles

*Waterfalls in Cat Gill, below
Walla Crag, near Keswick*

Waterfalls in Cat Gill, below Walla Crag, near Keswick

G reat Wood belongs to the National Trust, which has provided a car park shielded from the road by oak and beech. It is the first car park on the left-hand side of Borrowdale Road when driving from Keswick towards Borrowdale. Derwent Water lies blue and sparkling to the right.

In early May the beech are in delicate leaf but the oak buds are tightly closed. Hundreds of sessile oak have been planted by the National Trust on the slopes beneath Walla Crag where mature larch have been harvested. Below the tiny saplings are extensive carpets of violet, primrose and wood sorrel and each small gorse bush is ablaze with yellow flowers.

Willow warbler and marsh tit fill the woodland with their calls and occasionally a green woodpecker, after revealing its presence by its familiar "laugh", flies overhead and is soon lost to sight among the deciduous trees. Mallard wander through the fallen leaves, probably scavenging for scraps left by visitors.

A gate from the car park gives access to the path through the trees. Very soon, a signpost directs to Walla Crag or Ashness Bridge. The latter direction is the one to follow. A short walk leads to a rustic bridge crossing the beck. Here a huge bough hangs over the water, forming a natural seat for those brave enough to climb along it.

Cat Gill is a wooded delight but if the walker decides to clamber up, keeping close to the water, he needs to be fit and reasonably agile. There are grassy slopes on the south side of the beck and a well-trodden track. There are lovely views of Derwent Water behind and below to be savoured while getting one's breath back. The cackling of geese can be heard coming from the lake.

Soon the south side of the gill becomes too steep and it is time to cross the narrow, shallow beck just above a small fall where the rocks are fascinatingly stepped. Here a newly-made path keeps close to the water and rowan, birch and larch, all bedecked in new green, clothe the banks. The fern green spleenwort, bilberry and reed make up the ground cover.

Just where the beck seems to come out of a huge rock the gill turns at a right angle towards the north. Ahead lie tumbling waterfalls, sparkling like silver through the young foliage of the

A coal tit hangs upside down on a slender branch of larch.

larch. In the distance lies the steepest fall, but though it beckons with magic charm the sides of the gill become too precipitous for all but the young and the very athletic to continue scrambling through it. At this point the path turns and leads up the side of the gill. This recently-constructed path skirts the base of an unpleasant

51

slope of scree. At the top of the slope are new walls built by the National Trust and the colour of the rocks combined with the skill of the builder should be enjoyed before moving on.

From the path can be seen the deep fissures down which race tributaries hastening to swell the beck below. The sound of the water that drains off Low Moss fills the gill.

Just above the steepest fall on the beck a coal tit, in resplendent dress, hangs upside down on a slender branch of a larch. Under its weight, the supple twig bends gently over the great drop below. The white of the tit's nape is accentuated by the glossy, blue-black head and neck.

Above this fall the beck meanders through the open fell and just beyond it tumbles in a fan of white water, a pattern that is to be repeated all through Cat Gill until its journey's end in Derwent Water.

*Just beyond the open
fell the beck falls in
a fan of white water.*

*O.S. Map NY275208
1½ miles*

52

*Galleny Force and the
Waterfall in Greenup Gill,
Stonethwaite, Borrowdale*

Galleny Force and the Waterfall in Greenup Gill, Stonethwaite, Borrowdale

In late May, the woods bordering the Keswick-to-Borrowdale road are pale green with young foliage and the woodland floor is covered with bluebell. When the sun shines the blue of Derwent Water and the blue of the flowers exactly match. Near the village of Rosthwaite the valley opens out and the pastures support many sheep and lambs. Beyond Rosthwaite a left turn leads to the hamlet of Stonethwaite. There is parking space on a green verge on the right side of the lane before the cluster of houses and more parking in Stonethwaite itself. The houses are white and most are very old. The gardens are ablaze with flowers and swallow and house martin chase insects overhead.

The metalled road ends at the hotel but the route continues as a stony track. The fell towers upwards to the right and the oak, ash, hawthorn and holly-covered slopes are full of magpie, tit and chaffinch. Bird cherry is in full blossom and violet, celandine and primrose flourish below. Close by the path is an ash, where a willow warbler sings, its thin pointed beak opening and closing rapidly to allow the sound to fill the air.

Bird cherry is in full blossom.

Its tiny breast vibrates with each note of the descending scale of its song. Mistle thrush pass restlessly from tree to tree "churring" as they go, and meadow pipit flutter from rock to rock then ascend, trilling.

Where the rough road ends, by Alisongrass Hoghouse, a footpath carries on to Galleny Force. Here the Stonethwaite Beck makes a sharp turn. It plunges over a rocky ledge in a cloud of white spray, streaked with turquoise and deep blue. The drop is not great but the constraining walls on either side send a mist in all directions. The water enters a blue pool edged with oak and birch and is separated from another pool, equally deep, by a narrow rocky ledge. Both pools are suitable for swimming on hot summer afternoons. The Stonethwaite hurries on and swirls through narrow gaps and between huge boulders to fall in white tresses over another slope in its bed. On one of the huge rocks guarding this cascade is an oak, its roots entwining several boulders before it reaches soil. Perhaps the beck, fierce in winter, has washed away all the soil that once covered the boulders and the roots.

The narrow track continues and reaches the confluence of the Langstrath and Stonethwaite Becks. Picnic here and watch a male redstart that is using the bare branch at the top of an oak as a song post. It bobs and jerks and flits from branch to branch, always returning to its platform to sing its short, cheerful song. In the bright sun its black cheeks, grey back, chestnut breast, fiery tail and the white above its eye can all be seen. It was still singing when the writer, after a quick siesta, set off along the path on the west side of the Langstrath Beck.

Small blue butterfly flit across the path, they too enjoying the warm sun. Under a row of graceful larch with gently curving branches the beck tumbles in a series of white-topped falls and then flows over slabs of smooth, bleached rocks. Once past the trees the path continues through Langstrath to a footbridge that leads to the other side of the beck. Turn left and return along the beck, but this time on the western bank, until the Stonethwaite Beck is reached once more. Another footbridge crosses the Stonethwaite Beck and a track to the right leads through Greenup Gill. The slopes of Long Band that overshadow the east side of the gill are boulder-strewn, steep and scattered with hawthorn, now bright green. A male yellow hammer sings its familiar song from the top of the bush, its canary-yellow breast, chestnut back and streaked head very clear in the sunshine.

Small brown pools support flowering sedge and a host of pond skaters hurry across the surface of the water. Parsley fern, now lush and in large clumps, adds colour to the as yet brackenless fell.

Stonethwaite Beck waterfall

For most of its journey through Greenup Gill the Stonethwaite Beck is a waterfall. Its chattering fills the air and its tree lined sides soften the harshness of the west-flanking slopes of Bleak How and Eagle Crag. Just below the latter is a charming fall. Here, steep rock walls imprison the beck. A large projecting boulder divides the water as it rages over a sharp drop, forming two races white with foam. The foam is immediately lost as the water falls into a dark pool. Rowan and birch create the shade. Beneath these trees, bilberry, moss and liverwort grow. In the grassy slopes leading to the fall, violet, wild strawberry and the pale-green leaves of butterwort are seen. Overhead, a male kestrel hunts for prey and all around wheatear call and flit from rock to boulder.

Eventually the decision has to be made to leave this secluded peaceful gill. Return to the last bridge crossed and then follow the Stonethwaite Beck along its eastern bank, accompanied by pied wagtail feasting on a myriad of black flies that have hatched in the afternoon sun. Tree pipit flutter up from the scattered hawthorn. They parachute down with wings and tail outspread, uttering their distinctive, plaintive calls. In a wall near several ancient yew a wren is nesting. Its song drowns the gaiety of the tiny beck below.

On the return walk Galleny Force lies hidden beneath oak and soon the beck is lost to sight as the path passes beneath a tall, drystone wall. On the other side of the path is pasture, with a few scattered oak. Here three cuckoo disport in the sun. Two call in triplicate — "cuck, cuck, cuckoo." Two males chase the brown barred female. They alight, ungainly, in an oak, one bows forward, drooping its wings and fanning its tail. Then one grey bird, long-tailed and sharp-winged, chases the other and they dive and turn at hedge height, their barred undersides shining silver grey. They call and call, moving away towards the gill. A great spotted woodpecker drums continually, always from the same direction, unconcerned by the noisy courtship and rivalry taking place around it.

Leave these amorous cavortings and pass through the two gates to the bridge and across the Stonethwaite Beck. From here a farm lane leads into the hamlet. Here a welcome cup of tea can be bought at the tiny Peathouse Cafe. Drink it outside in the shade of the small cottage, listening still to the cuckoo and the woodpecker.

Cuckoo

O.S. Map NY273132, NY281122

5 miles

Waterfalls above Harrop Tarn, Thirlmere

O n a Spring Bank Holiday weekend, when the Lake District can be too full of visitors enjoying its glories, Thirlmere retains an air of peace and seclusion created by the empty waters of the reservoir: empty of swimmers, water skiers, little boats, larger pleasure steamers and ferries. The road on the west side of the lake passes close to the water and under tall beech covered with small, pale green leaves. It is free from the heavy flow of traffic that hurries along the A591. The parking space is ample on this side of the lake. For the walk to the waterfalls, leave your car just north of Dobgill Bridge.

Follow the sign for Harrop Tarn. Climb the stile, then follow the footpath which winds steeply upwards under

Young beech leaves and seedlings.

more beech. Below these grow bright green moss and young beech seedlings with glossy green seed leaves. Willow warbler carol from both sides of the path while the beck chatters noisily away to the left.

The beech is replaced by larch, with goldcrest flitting through the gently curving branches. The path continues to climb and passes through a clearing bare of trees because of huge rocky outcrops patch-worked with lemon lichen.

Beech replaces larch again and the "cheevi, cheevi, cheevi" song of the marsh tit joins the call of chaffinch and great tit. The sound of the falls in Dob Gill beckons the walker and a small diversion to the left leads to a natural viewing platform.

Beech seedlings.

Falls below Harrop Tarn.

When in spate the falls are spectacular. The white-topped water flows in great surges around islands of rock. It is streaked with brown as it reveals the peat stain. There are small side-races, swirling dark pools, tresses of foaming water and cascades all hurrying, urgently, down a rocky bed to reach the reservoir. Lining the banks of this fall are fern gardens with new fronds just unrolling, bilberry still in pink flower, huge mats of moss, leaves of sedge and dark bushes of juniper. Overhead the new leaves on sycamore and willow contrast sharply with the dark needles of Scots pine.

Rejoin the path after enjoying the falls and continue through fir where the ground is littered with large, fawn cones. The trunks are very tall and carry many dead branches. High up there is a dense canopy of dark green needles and little of the light or warmth of the sun reaches the stony track.

Where the path bifurcates, take the left-hand fork. A short walk leads to the edge of Harrop Tarn — an expanse of water the shallows of which are slowly being colonized by land plants. Turn left and follow the path beside the water, under more pine to a rocky ford which crosses the beck where it flows out of the tarn.

After several hours of heavy rain the water in the tarn flows quite strongly towards the ford. A sure step and a steady nerve will enable the walker to cross dry-shod. A stile gives access to the fell which is covered with juniper scrub, the haunt of goldcrest and stonechat.

Once past the juniper, cross the gently rising fell to the left to a cairn on Birk Crag. From here the whole of Thirlmere can be seen, with Skiddaw and Blencathra veiled in mist. To the south the pass of Dunmail Raise leads to Grasmere. On the other side of the lake the tree-clad lower slopes of Helvellyn, guardian of Thirlmere, are slashed with white becks. Overhead six buzzard wheel and soar effortlessly, their clear, ringing calls resounding over the fells.

From this glorious viewpoint return to the path and after crossing a barred fence turn immediately right, following a sheep track close

Stonechat

to a coniferous plantation. This quickly reaches the edge of the beck that has foamed through Ullscarf Gill. Picnic here, beside the chuckling, brown-stained water and sheltered by rocks that enfold the beck. Below, to the picnicker's right, the beck enters the forest through an arch of cypress, larch, spruce and pine, all resplendent with new growth.

Restored by a rest and a snack, take a sheep track that keeps close to the edge of the birch and rowan-lined rock cutting and, with care, view the racing water below. The small waterfall lies ahead. Two white streams race on either side of a large rocky outcrop. Then the beck idles in a shallow before tumbling down a long series of rocky steps, each ridge causing tiny white waves. It pauses again in a bubbling brown pool and then falls down more rocky steps into another deep, dark pool. From here it races into the rocky cutting, past a huge patch of wood anemone as white as the foam above.

This is a waterfall that hides coyly among the boulders. Its charm cannot be seen from the footpath only a few feet away, so the detour from the last stile is necessary.

The footpath comes to an abrupt end among pale pink violet, moss and bleached grass at the bottom of Ullscarth Gill. To climb the gill is well worth-while and there are sheep tracks to follow easily, past bilberry covered with delicately tinted berries. At the top of the gill a solitary rowan guards the beck just before it slides tempestuously down a rocky slipway. Cross the beck and the rather wet ground to the right. All the becks cutting through the deep peat moss are negotiable and the sphagnum-covered ground, though wet, is not treacherous.

From the top of Tarn Crags, enjoy the wonderful view of Thirlmere and Harrop Tarn. Just above the pine surrounding the latter, a buzzard is being harried by a pair of crows.

O.S. Map NY314132
4 miles

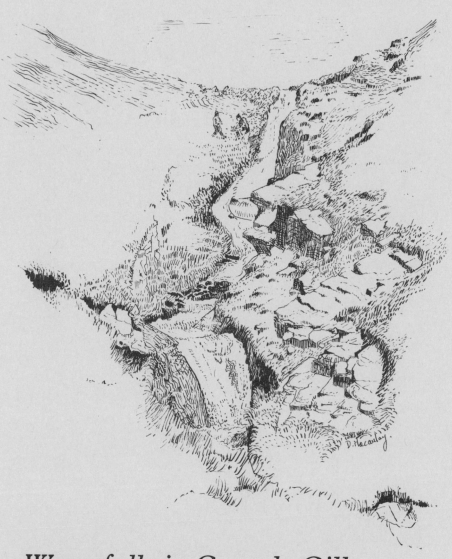

Waterfalls in Gasgale Gill,
Crummock Water

Waterfalls in Gasgale Gill, Crummock Water

The glorious walk to the waterfalls, deep in their mountain fastness, should be attempted in bright sunshine. Park at Lanthwaite Green Farm, where there is plenty of space for cars. In early June, willow warbler in trees beside the car park proclaim their territorial rights. The track through Gasgale Gill leads off on the other side of the road opposite the car park. Tormentil covers the ground beneath the newly unfolded bracken and a cuckoo calls from the direction of Loweswater. Cumulus clouds cast fleeting shadows on the fells.

Through the gill, the River Liza is narrow and shallow. Two simple steps on rocks take the walker across the water to the path on the north side. The steep slopes rear up on both sides and in crevices, among the layered Skiddaw slate, flourish clumps of parsley fern, the star-shaped rosette of leaves of butterwort and a rowan.

By the first fall on the beck, exposed quartz crystals sparkle in the sunlight and

Lower falls

tiny asplenium fern and milkwort soften the harsh environs of the path. In the quietness of this secluded gill the sounds of the beck rebound off the steep rock faces of the confining crags.

The path is easy to follow and rises slowy to pass below Gasgale Crags. The walker senses rather than sees Dove Crags on the north side of Grasmoor, because he catches only fleeting glimpses beyond the intervening scree slopes of the gill. Bilberry and heather colonise the scree.

By a huge boulder the path joins a higher path along the gill and enters a small plateau where meadow pipit flutter down from rapturous flights into warm air. A pair of crows nest on crags high above. Many of the rocks are stained with iron and glow in the sun. Wide green swathes sweep down the screes on the south side of the beck. These are the moss-covered banks of feeder becks streaming down the slopes to join the Liza. From the north side, a narrow beck hurtles down a gill below Hopegill Head.

Then the path turns slightly and there ahead lies the first waterfall. It negotiates a narrow cleft to fall into a shallow pool. It pauses momentarily, then drops in a curtain of water into another pool. Next, it slides over an algae-covered shelf and races around a rocky hindrance to plunge in two jets before it is channelled between the straight sides of a small rock cutting. To the left of the waterfall, screes stretch upwards to an arresting skyline. To the right, the slopes are grass-covered and sheep with lambs graze. A convenient flat rock by the water's edge makes a good picnic site, a place to enjoy the sun, the peace and the solitude.

The path continues to a second waterfall. This seems to advance from the top of the ridge in splashing cascades. The water then surges to the left around a large boulder and eventually the torrent races down a long slipway in a mass of white spray. Each droplet of water seems to catch the sun and dazzle the eye. After idling for a short distance, it repeats its passage along another rocky slipway.

From the top of the waterfall a wheatear scolds, anxious to divert intruders from its nest. Look back from here along Gasgale Gill and see the Irish Sea, pale blue in the misty distance, constrasting with a blue patch of Crummock Water below.

The path, continuing upward, keeps close to the Liza and soon Coledale Hause is attained. The view from here is unsurpassed. The Pennines are a grey smudge in the distance. Nearer lie Skiddaw and Blencathra and immediately below the mine road travels up from Braithwaite, with Keswick spread out beyond. Skylark rise and swallow chase flies.

It is always a joy to trace a beck to its source. Follow the ridge south, keeping Grasmoor to the right and Eel Crag to the left, and see the rise of the Liza. It originates among great springy hummocks of club moss, sphagnum, bilberry and sundew.

The ridge path traverses Whiteless Edge, and breathtaking views all around are revealed. Loweswater, Crummock Water and Buttermere are pools of dark blue towards the coast, beyond which are the uplands of the Isle of Man. Behind the walker are the Galloways and to the south lie the mountains of central Lakeland — Scafell Pike and its acolytes, all with every fissure and crag sharply delineated in the crystal-clear air. With the sun beating down, the gentle breeze is not enough to cool the brow on the climb to Whiteless Pike.

The path continues down towards Whiteless Breast. Bear right before Low Bank, keep to the path by Squat Beck and crossing Rannerdale Beck and Cinderdale Beck. From here a path beside the road leads upwards to the car park at Lanthwaite. On a hot day this is a long, uphill climb, but the peaceful lake to the left and the formidable crag of Grasmoor End give one ample reward.

Sphagnum/Sundew/Tormentil.

O.S. Map NY185215
NY188212 6½ miles

Waterfall in Ashness Gill,
Derwent Water

Waterfall in Ashness Gill, Derwent Water

O n a glorious day Barrow Bay car park might be full. The driver is then tempted to continue up the narrow road towards Watendlath, crossing the charming Ashness Bridge and leaving the car in Strutta Wood park. This road can become very congested and it seems wrong that the old bridge should have to bear such heavy traffic. Only one car can cross at a time so the jams are considerable. Perhaps it is better for one's conscience to leave the car in a park on the Borrowdale road and then walk through the wood to the bridge.

All the National Trust car parks are pleasant and families enjoy picnicking among the bluebells, beneath sycamore and birch,

Ashness Bridge

where the cuckoo calls and green woodpecker laugh.
Chaffinch, robin, blackbird, wren, tit, and jackdaw
abound and the chatter of the beck is ever present.
The path to the waterfall leads off the road,
opposite the entrance to Strutta Wood car park.
The beck lies to the left, with oak and birch
shading the tumbling water. Tormentil flowers
profusely in the turf and gorse is everywhere, each
bush a mass of golden blossoms.

Down by the beck a pair of grey wagtail
enjoy a break from domesticity. The female
preens on a rock and attends to her yellow breast
and creamy-coloured lower part and then each
grey wing feather is tidied. Next she preens her
long tail feathers and as she turns acrobatically
she reveals the bright yellow under her rump —a
yellow that matches the tormentil and gorse. The
male sits still on a nearby rock. Very occasionally
he flies to the beck or into the air to catch an
insect in flight.

Progress along the path is slow as the walker
turns frequently to enjoy the view behind.
Derwent Water and Bassenthwaite lie still and
blue below, with small tree-clad islands appearing
to float on the glassy surfaces. The sky above is a
deeper blue and cloudless.

On the brown hills beyond the lakes there is
little sign of the green mantle of bracken yet to
appear.

The path comes to some small falls where
streams of white water hurry around a silver
birch, the main trunk of which lies athwart the
bed. Small blue butterflies flit over the turf and
overhead two buzzards circle slowly, very high
up. Above the fell wall are heather, juniper,
scrubby hawthorn and small birch. A ewe and her
lamb rest in the shade of the trees. Deep purple
violet, wood sorrel, wild strawberry, milkwort and

Bluebell

69

*Streams of white water
hurry around a
silver birch.*

tormentil are all in blossom. Wheatear and meadow pipit dart
ahead. There are several paths, but that nearest the beck leads to
the bottom of the waterfalls. Ahead, the gill seems to come to an
abrupt end, blocked by the Dodd, a huge wall of rock in the shape
of a triangle resting upon one of its vertices. The sides of the rock
are green with young birch, ash and holly.

One final clamber along the boulder strewn path and a rocky
hollow below the fall lies to the left. If the beck is not too full,
stand in the hollow and look up at the great drop of water. The
white foam-flecked tresses of the waterfall plunge down a steep
rock face, stepped all the way down until they are deflected to the
left into a pool overhung by birch, ash, juniper and bilberry. The
water then rages around a craggy obstruction and piles up as it
enters a narrow cutting to cascade downwards in dozens of white
streams of water over more rocky steps and another projecting

boulder into a deep slit-shaped pool. The beck then flows over a ledge and topples in rushing white foam into a wide pool darkened by heather-topped steep rock faces.

At the bottom of the Dodd young aspen, still with reddish tinged leaves, tremble in a gentle breeze. To the left of the Dodd another beck drops in graceful falls through its gill until it joins the main beck. This gill is wider and receives more sun, and the tiny rock gardens are full of lush vegetation. There are grassy flats, too, just right for siestas, where scurvy grass, dandelion, violet and foxglove grow. There is an elm to shelter under if the sun is too hot. This is a secluded, serene meeting place of the two becks.

To see the top of the main falls, take the path out of the hollow and climb through the heather. The track keeps close to the gill edge and to the plummeting water after its rise below High Seat.

O.S. Map NY279194
2 miles

Waterfall on the Glenderamackin River, below Blencathra

Blencathra — or Saddleback, the name which aptly describes its shape — towers over the village of Threlkeld and dominates much of the first part of the by-pass from Keswick to Penrith. It is a mountain of riven rocks and scree, of dry river beds, of geological chaos. Many of us seeing its southern aspect hurry past, towards more familiar grandeur, missing the beauty that is hidden deep in its isolation.

One beauty is the waterfall found where the river Glenderamackin makes a large swing north to run between Souther Fell and Bannerdale. To reach this lively stretch of the lovely beck, park in the charming village of Mungrisdale, either by the phone box beyond the sign to the Mill Inn or by the post box set in the wall opposite the church. The latter is a long, low

St. Kentigern, Mungrisdale.

building, with cows grazing right up to its wall. A row of conifer shelters it from the icy winds that in winter must blow down the valleys on either side of the Tongue — a pyramid-shaped mountain close to the village.

Opposite the church and near the post box is a small clump of sycamore and alder and here a pair of flycatcher are busily catching insects and fetching berries for their brood. Their moss and lichen nest rests on a depression in the trunk of a sycamore. At some point the bark has

A spotted flycatcher feeding its brood.

cracked and a large piece has flaked off. The remaining bark, around the bare wood, forms a ledge for the nest and a shelter from rain over the top. Four fledglings sit on the exposed shelf-like nest easily visible to the careful observer and yet the gently stirring leaves of the tree and the drab coloration of their down feathers provide excellent camouflage. Only the orange of the mouths gaping wide when the solicitous parents arrive show that they are there.

If you have parked at the post box walk back past the church along the road to the phone booth, enjoying the cottage gardens, the lush buttercup meadows and the screaming swallow and house martin overhead. A path leads to the right past Bannerdale Cottage to a gate that gives access to a bridlepath once reinforced to carry traffic to and from the lead mines. On either side rushes flourish and below these tormentil and bedstraw. Close by, the mine road, after it has crossed Bullfell beck, sweeps off to the right below the Tongue.

Immediately the Bullfell is crossed leave the mine road and take a narrow track which runs beside the Glenderamackin river. It is sheltered to the left by Souther Fell, a towering mass of scree, barely covered with bracken and with a few scrubby trees. To the right the slopes sweep upwards, densely covered with young bracken. The beck chatters happily as it hurries over the rocky bed and its immediate slopes are colourful with foxglove in full bloom. Several pairs of wren are nesting along the banks, one under a grassy overhang where the river has washed away some of the peaty bank below.

The path is easy to follow but rather wet for nearly all its length until the confluence of the Bannerdale Beck with the Glenderamackin is reached. In a peat pool alongside the path, tadpoles, now large and green-brown — frogs all but for their tails —laze in the shallow water warmed by the hot June sun, undisturbed by a pond skater that scurries over the surface.

The ground on either side of the path becomes increasingly wet as the Bannerdale is approached and among the huge clumps of very wet sphagnum are the delicate pink flowers of cranberry. Above all this summery glory tower the formidable Bannerdale Crags, a rim of steep cliffs. They overlook Bannerdale, a silent and deserted vale now that the lead mines are disused. A buzzard circles overhead.

Cross the Bannerdale Beck, using convenient boulders. The path becomes a wide swathe of grass sweeping over the fell between the young bracken and stretching as far as the eye can see. Here on a Saturday at the end of June the path is all one's own. Only the birds disturb the wonderful seclusion. Meadow pipit, still resplendently speckled, call and trill in upward flight. Wheatear are seen and heard. But it is the whinchat that fill the

Foxglove

valley with their calls. A pair, stout and short-tailed, sit on top of bracken several feet apart and call. Their white eye-stripes are clearly seen and their yellow-pink breasts glow in the afternoon sun. Sometimes one disappears from its perch, to return in a few minutes with a mouthful of insects.

Small brown butterflies cross and recross the path. A pair flutter close together, settling to mate on a small patch of bedstraw. Where small becks bisect the path the lovely blue Skiddaw slate provides convenient stepping stones. All the time the Glenderamackin murmurs quietly in its rock-strewn passage and then is hidden from the path by rowan covered with blossom. Beneath, tiny falls send out their splashing sounds on the summer air. Where the rowan trees end the path comes very close to the beck and here the noise of falling water pinpoints the fall. It is so close to the path, and yet hidden among the trees, that it is easy to walk past, and that would be sad.

First enjoy the passage of the Glenderamackin, placidly traversing the open fell, and then cross the narrow beck by boulders — but not too close to where the beck suddenly drops down a very narrow gap between two huge squat rocks.

As the water falls, a large boulder divides the flow, which then comes together in a white plume to fall down a rocky chute, lined with moss and liverworts and bordered with bilberry, into a beautiful pool. This is clear, a deep slate-blue in colour and hidden in a hollow surrounded by rowans. The scent of their blossoms is very strong and it attracts many bees. Petals cover rush, fern, heather and the edge of the water. With care, climb down the slope and stand in the hollow and look upwards. Enjoy this graceful waterfall in its shady, remote hollow and perhaps on a very hot day swim in its deep, transparent pool.

O.S. Map NY346281
5 miles

Waterfall in Ben Gill, Ennerdale

Waterfall in Ben Gill, Ennerdale

L eave the Forestry Commission car park, which is situated east of Ennerdale Bridge and close to the western end of Ennerdale Water. The waterfall in Ben Gill can be seen high up on the west end of Revelin Crag. Continue along the road to the filter house and then pass through a gate to the track which leads through a meadow to the shore of the lake. Parts of the meadow are damp and here orchis and ragged robin bloom, and in the drier parts, clover, buttercup and bugle abound.

The path peters out by the weir, but the walker should continue for a short distance to a little footbridge over a marshy stream, white with the flowers of water cress and dotted with forget-me-nots. Close to the lake, several linnet seek seeds among the vegetation on the shore. All take off together and cross the meadow with a "lilting" flight, twittering as they go, and all that can be seen is their warm, chestnut-coloured back and a flash of reddish breast.

The shore of Ennerdale

At the gate in the wall below Anglers Crag is a National Trust sign. Young wheatear, keeping close together, settle on the wall. Then, as they flutter down to the pastures, their white tail feathers edged with black and their white rumps catch the sunlight. Once through the gate, turn right. The path leads uphill between a drystone wall on the right and a small fir plantation on the left. The fir are young and widely spaced and yellow hammer and wren call from the vegetation flourishing among them.

When the little beck is reached, turn left and Ben Gill towers upwards, with the waterfall sparkling and white at the top. The gill is a chaos of boulders and rocks, and over and around these the beck gurgles, chatters and tumbles. It flows through moss-ringed pools passing close to foxgloves and large clumps of heather blooming in rocky crevices.

Ragged Robin

An indistinct path, made by other brave souls who have climbed the gill, stretches a little way. But it is a case of clambering, hauling oneself up steeper boulders and climbing around others on mossy hummocks. There is always a way to surmount any obstacle in the gill. Take the climb slowly because it goes on for a long way. Half-way up, pause and enjoy the bilberry-covered slope on the other side

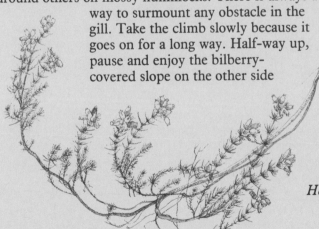

Heather

79

and the heather scattered on the rocky ledges all around. A large oak precariously hugs the cliff-face and above young aspen leaves quiver in the breeze.

Wherever a damp corner lies beneath one's boot, liverwort grow and the green of wood sorrel leaves and parsley fern relieves the bleached rocky desolation. Pass two large boulders to reach the lowest part of the waterfall. Here white water fans out as it is spread by the ridged surface of the rock bed. Another climb up the gill, this time over scree, and then a short clamber over bilberry and heather on the right of the scree brings one to a small pool into which two white jets of water drop. Between them the rocks are covered with moss and grass and one splendid shrubby hawkweed is golden-yellow in the July sun.

Aspen

Return to the scree and continue upwards. It is impossible to climb up at the edge of the beck as the rock face is too steep. After ascending for a short distance, cross the heather and bilberry where it is safe to do so. This brings the walker to the base of a single jet of water plunging downwards. Towards the bottom of its fall it is turned to the left and then to the right by narrow, projecting ledges to fall eventually into a deep pool shaded by rowan.

Once more return to the scree and struggle upwards. Again cross the vegetation to the right until the beck is reached. Here there is a pool bordered on three sides by overhanging rock. The beck is channelled through a shallow slip-way of its own making, then slides over a smooth, wide rockface in a curtain of white water. A last clamber up the scree, then a well-trodden path leads off to the right to the top of the waterfall. Follow the path around a jutting boulder and here take a well-earned rest, flat in the heather and in the full sunlight.

From this lonely, secluded nook at the top of the gill look to the left to see the beck ambling across the fell. Beneath one's feet it swirls around and under an overhang before it plummets downwards. Below, stretching downwards for a long way, is the gill. A corner of Ennerdale Water can just be seen. Common gulls wing their way from the lake to the seashore, perhaps Seascale or Ravenglass. Beyond the lake stretch the gentle pastures of north-west Cumbria. In the middle distance lies the Solway, blue and sparkling and even further away are the misty blue hills of Galloway.

Once refreshed, cross the beck and take the path to the right. This is easy to follow where it crosses the open fell. It leads to a stile on the edge of a fir plantation. Beyond the stile the path runs beside the wood, with the fell rising steeply upwards on the right. In early evening the path is bathed in sunlight and enhances the pleasure of walking downhill at last and on grass.

The path, always bearing west, reaches a wider part of the plantation and is lined on both sides by trees. Here the first fungi of the season grow under the pine. The shade is very deep but occasionally shafts of sunlight penetrate, and in these dance dozens of pale brown moths. Here no grass covers the path and the sound of footsteps is deadened by a carpet of conifer needles. At the end of the tunnel of trees, green turf can be seen again, and then a stile that leads out of the plantation.

Cross the stile and turn right and walk through the pasture between the rows of conifer and a drystone wall. Just before Crag farmhouse take the stile and ladder over the wall. An unmade road brings one back to the filter house and the car park.

O.S. Map NY088148
3 miles

Waterfalls in Launchy Gill, West Side of Thirlmere

To reach the magnificent waterfalls in Launchy Gill on the west side of Thirlmere, park in a bay opposite the sign for the nature trail. If this is full then park opposite the stile in the much larger lay-by 50 yards north of the sign. In the first week of July the road-side vegetation is lush. Bracken thrusts aggressively upwards but foxglove, deep purple vetch and cat's valerian, great opportunists, push their way through the fronds and colour the verges.

Climb the stile to where there is a box which claims to contain leaflets describing the trail — alas the writer has never found one. The path keeps close to the tumbling beck. It has recently been reinforced and where it comes to the edge of a small ravine it has been railed. Deciduous trees line the beck; they are a joy to walk beneath because, beyond the confines of the gill, conifer march for miles.

The next stretch of the path involves a strenuous climb. A tree marked with numbers lies ahead. A rocky path between conifer leads to the left below Thackmell Crags and to an enormous boulder left precariously balanced by the retreating ice, thousands of years ago.

Tottling stone

83

The grassy slopes around the Tottling Stone, as it is called, provide a first, splendid view of the reservoir, with Blencathra beyond. Here goldcrest and coal tit haunt the trees and gaps in the canopy reveal enough of the blue sky to allow the walker to catch a glimpse of a buzzard circling overhead and a pair of raven hurriedly returning with food for their brood on Thackmell Crags.

The path to the right of the way-marked tree provides an alternative route on returning to the car — but not yet, as the waterfalls lie farther up the gill. An indistinct path leads straight up from the way-marked tree. It becomes clearer and easier to follow after some 40 or 50 yards. The noise of falling water from the first fall directs the walker to a small promontory. From here the beck can be seen racing downwards in a flurry of white water.

First fall racing downwards in a flurry of white water.

The narrow path continues quite close to the steep edge of the gill: progress here should be slow and careful. The path leads to another promontory from which a spectacular waterfall can be viewed. The water squeezes through a narrow gap to fall in long, white strands. Fine droplets of water, sparkling as they catch the sunlight, create a continual mist as they ricochet off the many rocks that impede their downward way.

Below the viewpoint is a sunny hollow made for a sleep in the sun, a rare patch of grass uncolonised by the ubiquitous bilberry that covers the steep sides of the gill in a rich mantle of glossy green. Small whites and blue butterflies flutter over the open glade close to the water's edge. Oak and silver birch create a welcome but not too dense shade as the walker continues to climb. In these trees whitethroat and chaffinch call. The path, still very narrow and keeping close to the edge of the ravine, continues steeply upwards until a secluded, hidden valley is reached where grow foxglove, two kinds of mallow, heather, and tormentil with large yellow flowers, and where lichen cover the boulders.

A beck on the opposite bank of the Launchy drops vertically from a great height, having risen on Armboth Fell. It falls in a mass of white water and then joins the Launchy just before the latter makes the ebullient leap previously viewed from below. From here too the waters of Thirlmere and the fells beyond can be seen through a frame of silver birch.

After an easy scramble up the bilberry-covered slopes from this peaceful valley the walker regains the tiny track. Again care is required. Stop and enjoy the highest waterfall, which lies ahead, rather than walk and admire it at the same time. This is perhaps the finest leap of the lively Launchy. It rages through a narrow passage and then plunges boisterously into the secret valley, first in a jet to the left and then in white streams after swirling through a deep pool. It surges around boulders to spread into cascades as it encounters smaller rocks in its way.

A small conifer plantation on level ground is the backcloth for this lovely waterfall and the little path, still very close to the steep sides of the ravine, leads up and into it. Beyond lies the open fell and enough light enters the small wood for a soft carpet of grass to grow below the pines. The wood is a pleasure to walk through after the rocky path just climbed. Beyond the wood, the Launchy can be seen meandering across the open fell, a small beck giving few hints of its future impetuosity.

The fell is very quiet and stretches away towards Watendlath over a great wet moss.

Swirling through a deep pool.

Meadow pipit carol in the warm sun. Beneath one's feet the fell is dotted with small flowers; deep pink lousewort, dark-purple milkwort, lilac-coloured common speedwell, mauve butterwort and waxy yellow buttercup. Among the great wet mounds of moss is sundew, still in bud, but the leaves have been active and many a small fly has provided the missing minerals for this little insectivorous plant.

O.S. Map NY306156
2 miles

Barrow Falls, Derwent Water

Barrow Falls, Derwent Water

There are several ways to reach Barrow Falls, but to approach them by a lovely walk over the fells adds extra pleasure. Park again, as in early spring, in the National Trust car park at Calfclose Bay. In high summer the ground beneath the newly planted sessile oak is a mass of foxglove, meadow sweet, shrubby hawkweed and a white, long stalked, bedstraw, clambering where it can.

Pass through the gate at the back of the car park and follow the path that runs below Walla Crag in the direction of Ashness Bridge. This is well signposted. In July, the screeching of the peregrine chicks on the crag, as their parents approach with food, seems very loud. Cross the rustic bridge over the beck which is racing through Cat Gill. Here tree creeper sing their simple song and show off their white breasts as they search, acrobatically, for insects in the crevices of the bark of the oak shading the beck and bridge. Another sign points the way and the path leads from the trees in the gill and traverses the fell.

Below lies Derwent Water, with tree-clad islands, blue and placid in the sunlight. Only

Meadow sweet

the occasional cackle of geese disturbs its peace. Ahead is perhaps one of the loveliest views in the Lake District — Borrowdale, with one crag after another covered with deciduous trees, its valley bottom lush and its peaks high. These, now in shade and then in sunlight, slumber in the distance. The bracken on the fell is full-grown. Hawthorn bushes are covered with pale-green berries and in these yellow hammer call and great tit are busy hunting insects. Below, the leaves of the silver birch lining the lake shore move gently in a light breeze coming off the lake.

Along the becks that bisect the fell, lousewort, milkwort, common speedwell and rock stonecrop flourish and at last cross-leaved heath is in full bloom. After a short distance the path ceases to be a grassy swathe and becomes a rocky track, passing around boulders, climbing upwards and downwards, always delightful and easy to walk along. Beside the stony track white self-heal flowers. The path comes close to the perpendicular rock face of Falcon Crag, where young climbers are ascending on ropes, others are hurrying across the screes to join them, and the raven scold as they are disturbed by these two-footed, crab-like intruders.

Eventually, Ashness Bridge comes into view. Before the walker reaches it he must climb a ladder stile to the road from the lake to Watendlath. Cross

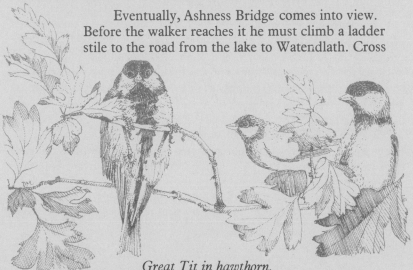

Great Tit in hawthorn.

the road, turn right and walk downhill for 100 yards or so. Then turn left before a drystone wall running off to the left. Walk around the intervening boulders, clumps of moss and rush and

Enjoy the view back along Derwent Water.

under the trees to the beck side. To the right is a weir, where the water of Barrow Beck pauses before it makes its first spectacular plunge in its haste to reach the lake. Stand here under a huge oak and enjoy the view back along Derwent Water to Bassenthwaite Lake and the Galloway Hills in the far distance. Skiddaw can be seen leaning benevolently over Keswick and the lakes.

From this viewpoint, slate steps lead downwards, between enormous rhododendron and foxglove, keeping close to the racing water. Herb Robert grows in the crevices between the steps. The beck leaves the weir and rages down a narrow rock slipway to fall in two jets into a wide pool that is so clear the large rounded rocks which cover its bed can be seen in every detail. In the dark recesses at the pool's edge, moss, fern, wood aven and juncus grow lushly in the humid atmosphere. The steps continue down, charmingly constructed, keeping near the tempestuous beck. Rainbows flicker over the spray as sunbeams are split into their constituent colours by the droplets. Honeysuckle clambers over tree branches and its blossoms perfume the air. Some trailing branches hang low over another pool. Then the water, tumbling vertically, falls on to projecting rocks and cascades, white-topped, lightening the shade of the vegetation.

The Barrow Falls, particularly after rain, are a wonderful sight. Viewed from the bottom they are quite breathtaking.

O.S. Map NY268199
3 miles

Waterfall below High Rigg,
St John's in the Vale

Waterfall below High Rigg, St John's in the Vale

There is plenty of parking space by the Castlerigg Stone Circle. The motorist approaching from Keswick on the Penrith road (A591) should take the first signposted right-turn. When aproaching from Ambleside on the A591, take a very narrow lane at the top of the hill just before Keswick. The circle, some 3,000 to 4,000 years old, is composed of nearly 50 rough-hewn stones. The tallest — taller than a man — makes a dramatic start to the walk to the waterfall on High Rigg. To the north-east lies Blencathra, its head in the clouds.

After pondering why the circle is where it is and what its function could have been, return to the lane and continue downhill from where you have left the car. Jay and magpie call from a small oak wood. Pass Goosewell Farm where elder trees are in full flower and the roadside verge is bright with pink campion, buttercup, St John's wort and meadow sweet.

Take the permitted path, well signposted, which leaves the road by some hawthorn trees. Here a common redstart flutters from branch to pasture with a fine display of its orange-red tail.

Castlerigg Stone Circle

The church of St. John's in the Vale.

The path, a short-cut, keeps close to a ditch bright with lesser spearwort, yarrow and forget-me-not. It then returns to the road by Naddle Bridge. Continue to the right along the road by a meadow. Over the wall are ragged robin, pale pink orchis and white campion. Then after two more right turns take the footpath signposted, "To St John's in the Vale and Tewet Tarn". The gate is beneath an ash tree laden with keys.

A track climbs obliquely uphill where skylark sing and pied wagtail flit across the pasture. Another gate gives access to rough fell, where only the moles seem happy. This is because of an outsize crop of thistle which are tiresome to man and his dog. Climb over throughs in a wall to where Tewet Tarn lies to the right, with the scudding clouds reflected in its still, clear water. Around its edges are pale white orchis, lousewort, ragged robin and bog asphodel just in flower. Among the reeds in the tarn is a mass of twigs left by a duck that has reared her young, all of them having departed.

Leave the tarn and pass through a gate. The path climbs gently uphill to Low Rigg where grow toadstools and pure white puff balls that as yet are not ripe enough to release their spores. A wall ahead, with throughs, leads to a grassy path between the low bracken and down to the church of St John's in the Vale. The wall acts as a hide, enabling the walker to watch a meadow pipit tend its foster child, a young cuckoo, four times the size of the pipit, screeching continually from a boulder. No piteous pleading this, but demanding and aggressive. The pipit works unceasingly to satisfy this huge bird.

She scurries under the bracken, running between the stalks, calling quietly to her youngster and then returning direct to the boulder to place some minute morsel in the large orange-coloured gape. She retreats quickly, still calling, as the young bird, displaying its barred breast and tail, flies low over the bracken to the wall. It lands in an ungainly fashion, too young as yet to handle its large wings well. Immediately the pipit is feeding it again and when she flies off to continue foraging the cuckoo flies after her trying to accost her as she goes. This time the fledgeling settles in the bracken and both are lost to sight, but their position can still be pin-pointed by the clamourings of the cuckoo and the reassuring calls of the pipit.

The church lies snugly under High Rigg and serves both the Naddle Valley folk and those of St John's in the Vale. The churchyard has seats and is sheltered from the breezes. Here there is perfect peace. Pause awhile and meditate on life as it must have been when those commemorated by the well-weathered headstones were alive and working. After leaving the churchyard walk westwards along the road and take a path immediately beyond the dioscesan youth centre. This is a steep path up the fell to a plateau. A gate on the far side opens on to a grassy path through the bracken. This is a joy to walk along. Up and up it goes to a small cairn on High Rigg. This is the territory of the wheatear and the meadow pipit and from here are spectacular views of the fells. Helvellyn lies to the south, with Thirlmere at its foot. To the west lie Grassmoor and the mountains around Newlands and Coledale, sharp and clear and delightfully shadowed by the fast-moving clouds. To the north are Skiddaw and Blencathra, steep and bleak with

Cuckoo chick fed by Meadow Pipit.

their tops now free cloud. To the east are the Pennines, pale blue and mysterious, and far away. Underfoot, the fell is covered with bedstraw, lady's slipper, tormentil and extensive mats of wild thyme.

The path continues from the cairn and comes close to a very long fell wall. At this point turn off to the right over the open fell and continue carefully to a higher, craggy area. Below, looking towards the south, in a hollow, lie two pools covered with the woolly white heads of cotton grass. These pools drain into a tiny beck that drops suddenly over a narrow ledge. This is the top of the waterfall and the high spot of the walk. With care, clamber down the north side of the crag beside the tumbling water and then cross the beck — only a pace wide — and look up at the long white tresses of water. They fall a long way, with spray bouncing off small ledges and ridges, each droplet sparkling in the warm mid-July sun. Brown Beck, as it is named, then flows across a small hollow to race down and down through the bracken.

Follow the beck down, crossing from side to side to walk along sheep tracks. Finally, a track passes under a copse of trees and here Brown Beck plunges exuberantly down a steeper slope in a mass of white spray. Follow the track to the left through the bracken and then clamber down to the road below.

Turn right along the road and follow it when it bears left towards Naddle and Dale Bottom. At the caravan site, take a footpath to the right, through the site to a gate at the end. From here an excellent track leads through gates, crosses the Naddle Beck, and continues on after throughs in walls and across sweet-smelling meadows to the A591. Only 50 yards of road walking need be endured before the metalled farm track leads to the right. Walk 50 yards and then strike out diagonally across the field just before Low Nest and behind a chicken house. Another stile admits to a metalled track to High Nest. A footpath continues when the road ends and this, after crossing several meadows, leads to the road and the car park.

Except for the descent from the waterfall and Brown Beck this is an easy, though lengthy, walk. But on a lovely sunny day and with a good pair of walking boots it can be attempted by the young and the not-so-young alike.

O.S. Map 305215
6 miles

Waterfalls in Dodd Wood, Thornthwaite Forest

I n August the roadside from Keswick to Dodd Wood, part of the Thornthwaite Forest, is bright with flowers. Rose-bay willow-herb dominates the vegetation but knapweed, wild parsnip, sneezewort, yarrow, angelica, fleabane, scabious and betony all grow in the colourful verges. The entrance to the car park in the forest is easy to miss while driving along the A591. It is signposted "Mirehouse historic house car park. The old sawmill tea room". Park immediately or bear right inside the entrance and drive fifty yards or so to the Forestry Commission car park.

The Ordnance Survey map shows waterfalls on Skill Beck as it flows through Dodd Wood and though there is no spectacular fall such as is found on the Dash, a short way to the north, the Skill is a series of small falls for all its length through the wood. The Forestry Commission, with the help of others, has established an excellent forest trail. From most parts of this trail, the walker can see the waterfalls. Leave the car park by a wooden bridge just below a weir shaded by sessile oak. Here herb robert and wood sage

'Knapweed' or 'Hardheads'

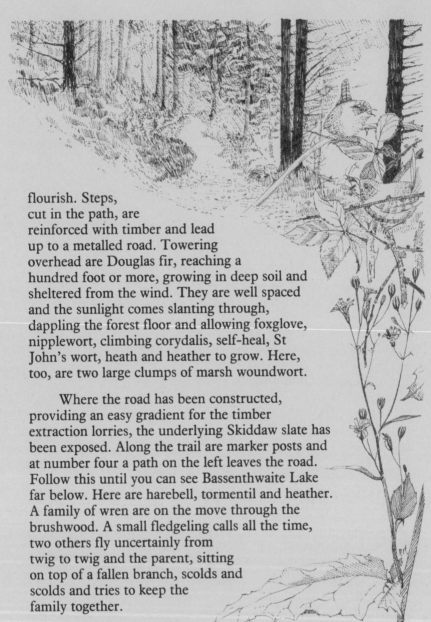

flourish. Steps,
cut in the path, are
reinforced with timber and lead
up to a metalled road. Towering
overhead are Douglas fir, reaching a
hundred foot or more, growing in deep soil and
sheltered from the wind. They are well spaced
and the sunlight comes slanting through,
dappling the forest floor and allowing foxglove,
nipplewort, climbing corydalis, self-heal, St
John's wort, heath and heather to grow. Here,
too, are two large clumps of marsh woundwort.

Where the road has been constructed,
providing an easy gradient for the timber
extraction lorries, the underlying Skiddaw slate has
been exposed. Along the trail are marker posts and
at number four a path on the left leaves the road.
Follow this until you can see Bassenthwaite Lake
far below. Here are harebell, tormentil and heather.
A family of wren are on the move through the
brushwood. A small fledgeling calls all the time,
two others fly uncertainly from
twig to twig and the parent, sitting
on top of a fallen branch, scolds and
scolds and tries to keep the
family together.

At station five, the path
makes a U-turn and passes between

*A family of wren
are on the move.*

young conifer, rowan and silver birch, all regenerating naturally. A flock of coal tit flit across a clearing, calling to each other. Overhead flies a buzzard, its clear, high call resounding over the forest. Pause on this part of the path and enjoy the views. Above lies the Dodd, where the use of various species of conifer avoids the uniformity that characterises so many Lakeland plantations. The summit is clad with mountain pine and noble fir. Beneath these are sitka spruce, a conifer with blue-tinged needles. Below again are the greener, more delicate branched European larch, then come another band of sitka spruce.

A long way down, more of the lake is seen and on the far side the forest-clad slopes and Lord's Seat, bold and bare. On either side of the path are delicious wild raspberries and great mats of heath and heather. Toadstools grow beneath saplings and a bright green willow warbler hunts among the leaves. Patches of bilberry are laden with their delicate flavoured fruit. To the left workmen can be heard using winches and "snigging" tracks.

The path turns and leads to the seventh station, where a small beck tumbles headlong down the steep fell. It fills the glade with noise as it hurries between beech on its way down the gill. It passes oak stumps scored by browsing roe deer and rowan now showing bunches of bright red berries. Here are more bilberry, with succulent fruit to quench the walker's thirst. Over the tree tops close to the lake a family of raven dive acrobatically and are lost to sight. The path enters a small plantation where juniper grows and beech trees nurse young larch. Coal tit abound. Three climb from the base of a trunk, pecking in the crevices for prey. Several hunt the forest floor, moving swiftly among the litter, examining every twig for insects. Their soft, incessant calls pin-point each bird as it moves quickly, its soft colouring making it difficult to see.

After this detour the trail rejoins the road for a few yards. Then take a right turn through the trees to a hollow and a footbridge over the Skill Beck. Pause here and enjoy the boisterous beck in its race through the forest. Continue through western hemlock and European larch which densely shade the path. Even here are birds. Goldcrest call quietly and a young speckled robin pleads plaintively to be fed by its attentive parent. Soon another forest road is reached.

The old sawmill tea room.

After a short walk, take the wooden steps down to the right by a stand of firebeaters. These lead to a path which travels beside the Skill at its most tempestuous. Here are foaming falls. The small beck seen earlier joins the Skill in a fan of white streams surrounded by large banks of liverwort, fern and moss. An island of rock parts the raging beck and two plunging falls send spray in all directions. Follow the Skill as it continues downhill. The path is heavily carpeted with needles, through which push fawn-coloured toadstools.

The trail finishes where it started by the bridge and weir and by the old sawmill tea room. While enjoying a delicious dish of bilberries and cream, look at the implements once used. The saw, now used as a counter on which to display china, was named "Jeannie" after the fiancee of the landowner who built the mill in 1880. The power to drive the mill came from the Skill Beck, which must have flowed as tempestuously then as it does now.

O.S. Map NY242278
2½ miles

Waterfalls in Sourmilk Gill,
Buttermere

Waterfalls in Sourmilk Gill, Buttermere

There is ample, if expensive, parking at Buttermere. Take the track to the left of the Fish Hotel. This is signposted to the lake. From this path can be seen in the distance the beck cascading down Sourmilk Gill. It passes between sheer rock faces in a long white plume of water dropping past large clumps of pink heather and delicately shaded by larch.

Take the left of the two field gates and follow a track bordered thickly with harebell on one side and pink persicaria on the other. Very soon the air is filled with the noise of the waterfalls and the water surging through Buttermere Dubbs on its way to Crummock Water. Another gate and stile give access to a water meadow and then a wooden footbridge over the Dubbs. Follow the track to the right and cross a wooden bridge which straddles the racing beck. Pause to look up at the water hurtling furiously on its long journey through the gill to join the water in the Dubbs. Continue across the bridge and after a few steps along the path beside the lake strike up to the right through Burtness Wood. A path through the trees has been constructed by the National Trust, sponsored by the Countryside Commission. It is built of syenite rocks from the Ennerdale granophyre which, when wet, glow a rich pink-red. For as far as one can see this red rock ladder climbs upwards. It is well constructed and the walker can always find a convenient foothold.

Burtness Wood is full of fine sycamore, larch and birch through which filters enough light for bracken, moss, liverwort, foxglove, tormentil, polypody fern and toadstool to grow. In the trees close by the path a troop of young goldcrest quietly hunt for insects; some travel along twigs, others hunt in crevices of the bark

Young goldcrests

and all the time they utter
their high, thin call. Near the edge
of the wood bilberry, with its succulent,
tart berries, grows. A stile gives access to the open
fell and bracken, heather and tormentil.

The path of flat, red stones still marches
upwards. This part of the path was laid under the
upland management scheme of the National Park
Authority. It makes for easy access to the waterfalls
at the top of Sourmilk Gill but was laid to take the
public away from the side of the steep gill after it
had claimed two young lives. On either side of the

Look back at the wood and Buttermere below.

path clumps of clubmoss thrive between heather and parsley fern. When in need of a rest, pause and look back at the wood and Buttermere below. To the right, Fleetwith Pike stands guard at the head of the lake. To the left, Whiteless Pike towers over the far bank of Crummock Water.

Refreshed, climb on up the steep red path. Above, the screes below High Stile glow warmly, with great mats of heather. Beside the path crowberry bears juicy fruit, and large clumps of Alpine Lady's Mantle are covered with delicate lemon-coloured flower heads. Wren scold from low-growing bracken and overhead there circles a solitary crow. The fell becomes even steeper and the wide path zig-zags to ascend. It then flattens out and swings away to the right along a grassy shelf to the side of the gill. More bilberry grows here, brightened by the tiny white flowers of eyebright. At the meeting of the track and the beck a grassy-covered boulder juts out over a waterfall. Stand here and look down on the heather and larch-clad gill and the foaming cataract, just as you looked up from far below. On the steep sides of the gill grow young larch, self-set.

A little way beyond this projection the path comes to the bottom of another fall, this one a spectacular flurry of white streams with spray tossed into the air as the great mass

Lady's Mantle,
Crow Berry,
Harebell.

of water bounces off large rocks and boulders that lie across the bed. Cross on the stepping stones to the other side. Follow the path to the left when it divides, passing through a broken-down drystone wall to Bleaberry Tarn. Sit here beneath the steep slopes of Red Pike and High Stile and watch the water gently lap the side of the tarn. The mist flirts with the fell tops, sometimes covering them and then lifting to reveal Bleaberry Comb and the tops above.

From this quiet pocket of water flows the beck that falls down the gill like cream — giving it its name, Sourmilk Gill.

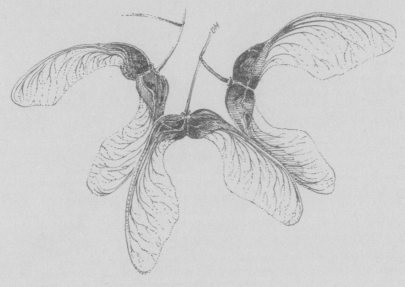

Sycamore keys

O.S. Map NY169158
3 miles

Waterfalls in Beckstones Gill, west side of Bassenthwaite Lake

In mid-September, swallow fly low over the car park at the edge of Powterhow Wood. The leaves of the beech, hazel and sycamore are faintly tinged with autumn colours and the bracken is beginning to fade. But bindweed, its large white flowers strategically placed on the top of the bushes, thrives aggressively. Below in the thickets, a robin sings a sad, tender song. Towering over the car park and the nearby Swan Hotel is the large, inhospitable, pyramid-shaped Barf, a shoulder of Lord's Seat.

To reach the waterfalls, cross the road and follow the metalled track into the woods. After a hundred yards or so, leave the track by the second stile on the right. This gives access to a glade of silver birch and larch, with lush grass underfoot. Here thrive toadstools of all colours and sizes but the eye is caught by the brilliant scarlet caps of numerous fly agaric.

"The Clerk"

Among the trees is The Clerk, a small pinnacle of slate little taller than the bracken and starkly white. Above, high up on Barf, is another slate projection, many times larger than The Clerk. This too stands out, unnaturally white, and is visible for many miles. Both The Clerk and The

"The Bishop"

Bishop, as the latter is called, are kept white-washed by the landlord of the Swan Hotel. Legend has it that a Bishop of Derry and his horse are buried below The Clerk. The Bishop, while on his way to Derry by way of Whitehaven, accepted a wager in the inn to ride his horse to the top of Barf, and the large whitened pinnacle marks the place where the horse stumbled and both died.

Follow a green path that keeps within earshot of the beck on which the waterfalls lie. At times it passes among gorse and bracken. When it comes to the water's edge, cross to a path on the other side. This path, made by sheep and walkers, climbs upwards between the forest fence and the beck. Sometimes it is easy to follow. At others the walker has to struggle through head-high bracken. Occasionally a rock hinders progress and the walker must clamber carefully around it. But it is possible, if wearing stout boots, to climb the length of the gill, keeping close to the chattering water which flows from its source near Lord's Seat.

Soon the bracken edging the path gives way to bilberry covered with large, deep-blue fruit. On the other side of the beck towers the steep desolate scree slopes of Barf. The shattered slate comes right down to the edge of the beck, colonised only by clumps of parsley fern, foxglove and, here and there, a young larch. High above, where the slopes are less sheer, bracken and heather soften the stony chaos. A few hundred yards along the

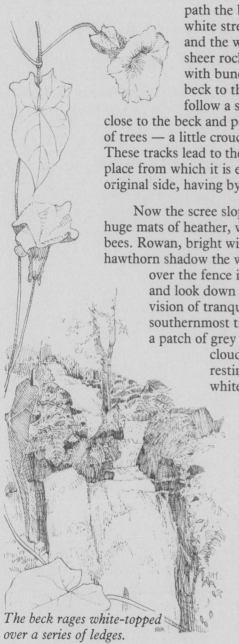

path the beck drops in a fan of white streams as it leaves a gorge, and the walker is confronted by a sheer rock face. Below an ash laden with bunches of keys, cross the beck to the opposite side and follow a sheep track that keeps close to the beck and passes under low branches of trees — a little crouching is required here. These tracks lead to the water's edge and to a place from which it is easy to return to the original side, having by-passed the rock face.

Now the scree slopes of Barf are pink with huge mats of heather, which are paradise for bees. Rowan, bright with red berries, and hawthorn shadow the water. Pause by a stile over the fence into Beckstones plantation and look down on the Vale of Keswick, a vision of tranquillity, and at the southernmost tip of Bassenthwaite Lake, a patch of grey reflecting the storm clouds above. Just above this resting place the beck rages white-topped over a series of ledges. It falls to the right and to the left in a wide curtain of foaming water under a large holly tree. The beck then plunges down a long, rocky slipway which is edged with wood sage, honeysuckle, mounds of trailing moss, fern and rush. It fills the gill with noise.

Follow the faint path carefully until the beck flows through a

The beck rages white-topped over a series of ledges.

narrow rock cutting. Here among rowan, larch and juniper, with heather, tormentil and fern underfoot, the beck plummets in a wide spread of streams into a fern-ringed pool. Coal tit stridently call from larch close by. A few more yards and the highest waterfall is reached. Here the water rages downwards in a long white jet between golden rod and then falls in foaming cascades through heather, fern, moss and liverwort — a lushness that contrasts strikingly with the now almost barren scree above.

After a picnic on the grassy sward at the top of the fall, take the stile over the fence into the forest and walk a short way along a forest ride, looking immediately for the first path that drops down among the spruce on the left. From here the way is downward and easy to traverse compared with the arduous climb through the gill to the waterfalls. Rocky steps help the walker down a small rock face in the plantation. Along the side of the path, heather and wood groundsel flower and robin, wren, bluetit and blackbird call.

O.S. Map NY213265
2½ miles

Waterfalls in Roughton Gill, Caldbeck Fells

Waterfalls in Roughton Gill, Caldbeck Fells

It is a glorious experience to journey in late September from Penrith along the A66, through Mungrisdale and Hesket Newmarket, to Fell Side, or from Keswick on the A591 through Orthwaite. Hazel lining the roadside are now covered in golden leaves; silver birch and ash have pale lemon banners; sycamore and horse chestnut leaves are tinged with brown; hawthorn are a rich plum colour and rowan, the gayest of them all, is a riot of rich reds and gold.

At the hamlet of Fell Side take the turning beside Fell Side Farm and use the wide verges above the farm buildings for parking. Beyond, the metalled road leads to a gate and a stile that gives access to a rough road that was much in use when the mines on High Pike were being worked.

The route to Roughton Gill is well signposted beyond the stile. To the left the fell stretches upwards covered with ripened grass. To the right, over the drystone wall, are the well managed fields of the farm, neatly hedged or walled.

After half a mile the wall and the fields are left behind. The unmetalled road leads into the depths of the softly rounded hills now tinged with red where the tiny leaves of the low growing bilberry are showing their autumn colours. Over the yellowing grass flit a small flock of young meadow pipits twittering as they go.

There is a ford and a footbridge over the Ingray Beck which merrily tumbles between rocks covered with bright green moss. It is on its way to join Dale Beck which flows through the valley bottom.

Continue along the track, which soon comes close beside the Dale. The edges of the track are still bright with marsh thistle, hawkweed, yarrow and spearwort. The fell on either side is steeper now and the lower slopes are golden brown with dying bracken. Above the bracken the rounded tops are covered with grass with no rocky outcrops to break the smooth lines. Ravines cut down through the slopes and are soft of line and colour.

The Dale Beck chatters as it goes and is foam topped as it swirls around boulders. Another footbridge enables the walker to cross to the other side of the stream dryshod. Follow the track until it comes near to the bottom of Roughton Gill. On the left bank are huge mounds of gravel and mine spoil only very slowly being softened by nature.

Take a narrow path along the right bank of the ravine. To see the lowest waterfall leave the path at the entrance to the gill and walk a few yards to the edge of the gorge. From here there is an excellent view of a long white jet of water deflected by a huge boulder near the top of its impetuous leap. Over the elegant fall leans a graceful rowan laden with a lush top of berries.

Continue along the little path, bordered with thyme, as it climbs beside the dancing water to a secluded grassy flat. Here, deep in the fastness of the hills, the walker can picnic and take a long look at the racing water and the glorious rowans that border its right edge.

Cross the beck and begin the exciting scramble upwards. Just by the lowest of a series of charming cascades is a dark cave.

Yarrow

113

This is an entrance to an old mine-level. Above this dark hole in the mountain face are convenient rock steps to help one's ascent to another mine-level entrance, this one still bearing traces of timber sleepers used, perhaps, for sledges carrying the ore.

Higher up still is another delightful grassy area with steep rock faces towering upwards covered with bright red bilberry and the yellow flowers of biting stonecrop providing a striking contrast. Beyond the greensward lies the highest waterfall in the gill. Two long streams of water drop over a lip of rock having been divided by a huge boulder athwart the ledge. These two graceful streams plummet downwards past moss and liverwort into a shallow pool before rushing on to descend the gill. Raven call from the slopes of Great Sca Fell and then glide over the gill with effortless grace, using the rising air currents. A buzzard circles very high up, and for once is left in peace of the raven. On retracing one's steps on the return journey spend some time looking at the mixture of ores among the gravel covering much of the east side of the gill. Here is white quartz, green copper and blue, reminding the walker that Roughton Gill once contained a very rich mine that gave up many treasures from its inner recesses.

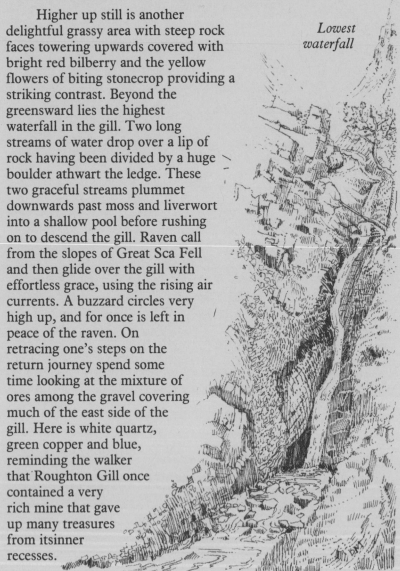

Lowest waterfall

Waterfalls in Wythburn Valley, Thirlmere

Waterfalls in Wythburn Valley, Thirlmere

There is a small car park at the southern end of the minor road that runs along the west side of Thirlmere. In late September the ash and rowan growing around the park are tinged with yellow. A robin sings from the lower branches of a conifer and another chases it away. Blue tit and great tit hunt among the needles for food. A tree creeper, with a sparkling white breast, three times ascends the trunk of the same tree in search of prey. Blackbird pass across the park clearing and chaffinch forage near the car for crumbs.

Buzzard flying to conifer

Leave the car park and turn left, crossing the bridge. Then take a gate that gives access to a permitted path across the meadows beside the beck. Steele End Farm lies away to the left, partly hidden by tall trees which shelter it from the winter winds that must sweep down the valley. Ash and willow line the beck and when it is in spate the water swirls around their roots. Pass through the first gate ahead. Its protective sycamore is showing brown along the edges of some of its leaves. The path continues, keeping close to the swiftly flowing water. The bracken on the far side is almost completely brown.

Beyond is a drystone wall that has collapsed in several places. A buzzard flies low over the pasture to the left and then moves into the plantation nearby and settles in a conifer.

At the next wall is another gate and a ladder stile. A few stunted Scots pine grow widely scattered over the fell. From out of the mist flirting with the crags above come foam-topped becks racing down from Steel Fell. Occasionally a meadow pipit flits ahead of the walker and a pair of crows circle over the valley and are quickly lost in the mist. Pass through the next gate and notice the lesser spearwort growing in the marshy ground. Bog asphodel is now quite dead. Among the heather, kept short by the sheep, lichen and red toadstools grow. Look up at the first sighting of the waterfall, high up, a wall of white water coming out of the mist.

Scattered along the beck are isolated willow and rowan. The latter are laden with a huge crop of red berries that brighten the greyness of this secluded, misty valley. The path leads through the last gate down to a sturdy bridge over the beck. Stand on the bridge and look up at the Wythburn racing furiously over its stony bed. To the left of the bridge is a well constructed wall alongside a grassy area which the sheep use for shelter from the rain and wind. Retrace your steps and beyond the sheltered area the path continues through the bracken but still in sight of the beck. Now the Wythburn is shadowed by silver birch, with their leaves just beginning to show a slight

*Rowan
berries*

yellowing. Tormentil blooms among the grass and parsley fern is very green.

The bridge over the beck.

The slopes of Castle Crag to the north of the beck are quite brown and all its bracken is dead. Above the bracken is a long wall and above all are barren crags. Below Black Crag, on the southern bank of the beck, much of the bracken is green and, here and there, young plants have just unrolled and show the freshness and vigour of June. Several foxgloves bloom close to the path. The path is now stony and very wet but it is easy to follow and walk along. The beck is a continual waterfall and the gill is full of the noise of rushing water.

Two becks hurtle down the steep slopes below Castle Crags, joining the Wythburn at the lower waterfall. The water crashes in a mass of foam against a buttress of rock. It roars through a gap beside this enormous boulder to fall in a jet into a white-topped pool. Two small side-falls also drop into the pool. The water races on into another pool that is dark and surging. It passes through a rock cutting, seething against the confining sides, beneath rowan and fern. A ring ousel lingers and when disturbed by the walker flies to the outcrops on the slopes above.

After a short, steep climb the path reaches the top of a rocky outcrop. Ahead lies the upper waterfall, a great wide curtain of water that comes roaring over the topmost ridge. Projecting boulders cause the water to cascade. Down goes the beck, in a white glory — a glory that is not obscured by trees. Only a few juniper grow here and these crouch beside and below the boulders flanking the beck.

The path, now more often than not a stream, keeps close to the wall of boiling water. At the top of the fall, a large grassy glacial mound stands like a guardian of the beck.

This is a splendid walk, but after rain it can be very wet underfoot. Good strong footwear is a must.

Juniper

O.S. Map NY307116
3½ miles

Waterfalls on Kilnhow Beck and in Gate Gill, Blencathra

Take the A66 from Keswick and turn left at the first signpost to the village of Threlkeld. Once in the centre of the village take a right turn leading to the school and the Blencathra Centre. On the right, a few hundred yards past the school, is a car park provided by the Lake District National Park. From here a well-defined path leads up towards Blease Gill and the first waterfall of the walk. Sit on a conveniently placed bench and enjoy the view of the village below and the fells beyond. Then set off along the path, which is enclosed by drystone walls and brambles loaded with fruit. Robins serenade the warm October sun and a green woodpecker hurries away from the trees toward High Row Farm.

Tormentil flowers underfoot and rowan berries catch the sun. These are irresistible to mistle thrush, which move noisily through the trees and then fly off with a grating churr, leaving many berries strewn below. The Kilnhow Beck, on which the waterfall lies, negotiates its stony bed cheerfully as it flows through a tree-lined gully. Many sycamores lean over the beck, and it sparkles in the light now that the sun can reach through gaps left by the falling leaves. Where bracken borders the path and the beck, some fronds are tinged with brown, but shrubby hawkweed and lesser stitchwort are still in flower.

On another seat, strategically placed by the Friends of the Lake District, sit again and enjoy the view. Threlkeld Knotts and Red Screes lie directly ahead and to their right are Low and High Rigg with Raven Crag in the distance. The path drops to a plank bridge across the beck, and from here the waterfall can be seen making its way beneath the trees into a pretty dell. Cross the bridge and walk along the side of the beck. Recross the water by a

convenient rock and walk a
few feet along the left side
to the edge of the hollow
below the fall. Here the
water is silvery in the
sunshine as it falls
over a ledge
between bracken
and hazel. A sycamore
spreads its branches over
the beck as the water races
white-topped over stepped
rocks to fall in long tresses.
These drop into a clear
pool with a pebbled bed. A
dark green blanket of liverwort
covers the rock behind the main
fall. Bracken, with no sign of autumn
tints, and rushes, kept continually
damp by the spray from the fall, grow
lushly in this secluded dell.

The bleakness of Blease Gill and
Knowe Crags contrasts sharply with the
rich vegetation of the dell, the alders that
line the banks and the larches beyond.
Return to the path that continues beyond
the bridge between the wooded slopes of
the beck and a sturdy drystone wall. At the
gate, turn right. Follow a track that keeps close
to a wall running across the broad base of
Gategill Fell. Above stretches pasture covered
with dead bracken and beyond the fell wall the
steep slopes are grey-brown with dying
heather. A painted lady flutters across the track
and settles on a sun-warmed slate. A large hare
crosses ahead on the path and it too rests in the
sun well up on the slopes, unconcerned by a
pair of buzzard slowly quartering the fell, their
ringing calls travelling far through the still,
clear air.

*A green
woodpecker
hurries away
from the trees.*

At a ladder stile, pause on the top and look back at the western fells, each peak, ridge and valley startlingly clear. Continue across the pasture to a gate in the wall. From here is an excellent view of the waterfall on Gategill Beck. The beck flows past spoil heaps from ancient mine workings below slopes sparsely covered with yellowing grass before it starts its leap into the valley below. First it dashes down a long rocky slipway before falling in a wide sheet of foaming water into a very deep pool. Under a straggly rowan it swings to the right before making a great surge back to the left. Then beneath a single, splendid rowan it plunges again into yet another pool.

As the valley widens the water spreads out, flowing noisily over its stony route past a ruined hut. It negotiates a weir just before entering a wooded ravine with a small larch plantation to the east. Take the path on the west side of the weir. This leads to a gate and another Friends' bench. Again the latter is well placed, sheltered and sunny, just right for a quiet siesta, or for watching the coal and blue tit that abound in the trees close by. A reinforced path leads down to Gatehill, the sound of the beck accompanying the walker on his way to the gate at the bottom. Here are the kennels of the Blencathra foxhounds.

Follow the signpost directions for Threlkeld.

Waterfall on Gategill Beck

Notice the interesting mounting block outside the Horse and Farrier Inn. The inn has a sign above the door saying it was built in 1688. On the other side of the road is a gate into the churchyard and just beyond the gate, on the right, is a memorial to huntsmen. Their names and the ages are given, and many of them achieved well over their three score and ten years in the last century. Perhaps it was tramping the fells after the hounds that resulted in their longevity. A fitting sentence tops their names: "Around them stand the old familiar mountains." A pleasing end to an excellent day, with good views, good waterfalls and good walking.

Threlkeld Church

O.S. Map NY316258   NY324263
3 miles

Waterfall on Comb Gill Beck
below Bessyboot

Waterfall on Comb Gill Beck below Bessyboot

To reach this lovely secluded waterfall park at the Seatoller Barn car park. This is screened from the road by a row of rowan and in mid-October these are heavily laden with large bunches of vermillion fruit. Turn left out of the car park and walk along the small footpath beside the road in the direction of Stonethwaite. Once past the row of white houses called Mountain View cross the road where a gate leads to a signposted path that traverses a pasture to a drystone bridge over the Comb Gill Beck. The track, deeply rutted by a tractor, passes through ash and alder as it nears the hurrying water. These trees show little sign of autumn colours, unlike the bracken, now a rich russet brown, covering the lower slopes of High Knott.

Comb Beck, Bessyfoot

Cross the ancient bridge and pass through the gate directly ahead. If time is no object turn right and walk up a wide track beside the tumbling water to an old mill which has been pleasantly restored, leaving the huge iron and wood water wheel standing against the building, its base fixed in the bed of the stream and still splashed by spray. From the old bridge a track leads straight up the fell for a hundred yards or so before it turns right and crosses the fell well above the beck. If you have visited the mill this path can be reached by striking up the steepish grassy slopes, which are covered in parts by bracken and have a few ash and scrubby hawthorn. Wren scold from the bracken and young chaffinch play chase among the branches of the ash.

The path across the fell is sometimes rocky but grass grows among the boulders and there is no sign of erosion, evidence that few people use this route to the tops. After a hundred yards the glorious waterfall comes into sight. As the path approaches a tumbledown wall strike downhill through the bracken to a huge craggy boulder that acts as an excellent viewing platform for the impetuous beck.

Before its dramatic leap it divides into two streams. The one to the right races among boulders and below a drystone wall before it plummets in long white strands of water. It drops into a foaming pool ricocheting out to fall in white topped tresses over tiny ledges. It races on, foam topped, down a rocky slope into a boiling pool. The fall to the left is channelled between the steep sides of a small ravine. These confine the water so that it foams like cream as it bounces from one rocky step of its bed to the next, before it drops into a deep turquoise pool. The racing water is then divided by a buttress or rock. Once around this the water from both pools unites to rage on through a necklace of blue-green pools that carry the water on down the silvan gorge.

Water Wheel

127

Silver birch with yellowing leaves, and rowan with more berries than leaves, line the banks of the fall and stretch up to the top of the steep slopes behind. Return to the footpath and look back at the glories of Borrowdale flanked by the Jaws, with Derwentwater, blue and peaceful, in the distance. Pass onto the open fell by a gate in the wall, noticing the hinge set into the enormous boulder used as a gatepost and musing on the effort that must have been required to put it there.

An indistinct path leads across the fell. Below, the beck slides over rocky slopes in a boiling mass of foam. Cross a tiny beck that bisects the path and then ascend the grassy slopes that sweep steeply upwards on its southern bank. Brightly coloured toadstools spangle the turf and spearwort and self heal still flower. Try not to miss the very narrow but steep fall of water in the little gill. Climb down the gently sloping sides and look up the tiny ravine lined with rowan rich in berries. Foxglove and heather bright with flowers and lush green ferns fill this hollow with colour and make it ideal for a picnic.

After leaving the secluded hollow continue upwards. From here it is just possible to see the top of the large natural cave, now dangerous because of extensive rockfalls, in the side of Dovenest Crag on the eastern flank of Comb Gill. Comb Door is silhouetted on the skyline.

Tarn at Leaves

Once the plateau area above the gill is reached follow a faint path that swings upwards and away to the right between two great craggy outcrops. This takes one into the territory of the raven, and pairs wheel acrobatically overhead calling to each other with deep croaks. This last ascent seems almost one too many and then, once over the brow, Tarn at Leaves is seen below and makes all the hard climbing worthwhile. This delightfully named stretch of water lies in a hollow surrounded by lichen-covered, jagged-topped grey crags. The surface of the tarn is tranquil and reflects the soft clouds scudding across the blue sky. Sedge grows thickly around its shore. Only sheep tracks lead to the tarn edge.

Return down the side of the little gill and then cross the main beck by convenient boulders. Turn right and follow the wide rocky track that sweeps through the trees seen earlier above the waterfall. On this side of the beck it can be heard falling noisily, its glories remaining hidden by its wooded surrounds and the steep sides of the cleft. This path eventually reaches a ladder stile that gives access to a lane and the main road. From here it is a quarter of a mile to Seatoller.

O.S. Map NY253131
3½ miles

Waterfalls on Woundell Beck and Low Beck, Ennerdale

There are delightful waterfalls at various stages of this walk. In between, the long, glorious trek which takes you to the heights demands a steady nerve and requires fitness and energy. At the end of the day you will be tired but uplifted as only the hills can make you feel. Leave the village of Ennerdale Bridge by a turn signposted Ennerdale Water, then take a left turn signposted Croasdale. At Whins, continue on to the lake and leave the car in the Forestry Commission's car park. The hazel, birch and bracken that line the winding lanes are now quite yellow and the golden glow is a foretaste of much to come. Bowness Knott towers over the car park and the needles of the surrounding larch trees drift continually down on the vehicles and walkers, covering the ground in a lemon carpet.

The spectacular view ahead

The forestry road keeps close the lake, with its mallards, and passes larch plantations aglow with autumn tints and pine trees dark and sombre. Here and there a copse of beech flames bronze in the morning sunlight. Along the roadside scabious, bedstraw and gorse still flower. The two-mile walk to the bridge across the Liza is hardly noticed because of the spectacular view ahead. Steeple, Pillar, Haycock and Scoat Fell rise gamboge-coloured above dark conifer plantations. Beyond the bridge a rough road takes the walker to the south side of the lake. Turn left to another road and cross the Woundell Beck. Then turn right along a narrow track that runs between the beck and a plantation where coal tit chatter unseen.

Follow the path as it moves into the trees, but not away from the noise of the chattering beck. By two trees way-marked in blue turn right and walk down to the beck. Just to the right the water from Deep Gill and the Silverdale Beck unite to form the Woundell Beck. Both streams are crossed by wooden bridges and there are seats set among a glade of deciduous trees. Where the waters meet there is a pretty fall that tumbles past golden grass, golden fern and golden-leaved rowan. A large oak spreads its branches benevolently over this glorious corner that is aglow against a blue-green backcloth of spruce. When you can force yourself to leave this idyllic seclusion return to the path, climb a few feet to the forest road and walk along to

A pretty fall tumbles past golden grass, golden fern and golden-leaved rowan.

the right. The road ends, and a path continues uphill between
larch on one side and the lively beck in a small ravine below. The
slopes of the ravine are clad in multi-coloured birch, larch and
rowan and several holly laden with berries. To the right, a gap
between the trees reveals three lovely waterfalls. One is a mass of
white tresses and one a series of cascades, and the last leaps in two
long jets into a blue-green pool with large round pebbles at the
bottom.

Continue along the path, passing through a glowing glory of
larch on the left and birch on the right until the trees end and a
stile and gate give access to the open fell. A narrow sheep track
climbs through Deep Gill among heather and bilberry, keeping
close to the beck all the way. This is a long, tiring climb
but the beck and its delightful falls encourage one to
keep plodding ever upwards. Pause often and look back
at the lake below and the fine mountains beyond.

Another waterfall is reached, this one set among the
bleak slopes — a waterfall that makes its way in a
flurry of white water down a steep-sided
canyon into a clear,
deep pool. Here the few
rowan that manage to
survive are covered with
bright red berries.
Climb on through Deep
Gill, keeping Great
Cove to the right and
Haycock ahead and then
take the bank of the
left-hand tributary
where two becks
converge. By now the path
has faded but keep close to
the beck past a small fall.
Continue up and up,
taking a quick but
careful peep over
the edge of
Mirkiln Cove.

Falls on the Woundell Beck.

From here make for the drystone wall that strides across Haycock and Scoat Fell. The latter is a high, wide plateau covered with fir clubmoss, lichen and moss. Its flatness gives relief to one's tired legs that have been going upwards for a long time. It is a plateau for views. Cross the wall by a convenient gap and walk across the top. Wastwater Screes can be seen, but not the lake. Scoat Tarn, Low Tarn, Burnmoor Tarn and Eel Tarn are patches of blue far below. Black Combe to the far right, and the Scafells to the far left, are giants in the mist. Overhead a kestrel hovers, searching for a meal, and a pair of raven soar across the vast hollow between the peaks.

Return and cross the wall and walk towards the cairn at the start of the path that leads to Steeple. This is an exhilarating part of the walk. The path is good and well marked but the ground drops steeply to Mirkiln Cove on the left and even more steeply on the right to Mirk Cove. Eventually the tiny summit with its cairn is reached. The view downwards is of a chaos of rock, of buttresses, of crevices and of boulders riven and twisted into fantastic, jagged shapes. But the summit must be left, so follow the well-cairned path down Long Crag — again another exciting path to follow where the walker may find it useful to look for the next cairn before leaving the one just reached. On the slopes there is a profusion of fir and alpine clubmoss; cowberry, with the undersides of its leaves dotted and alpine lady's mantle, with all its leaves tinged with bronze. Large red boulders of the Ennerdale granophyre litter the fell side. Suddenly the path ends and the walker has to scramble over heather to a stile in a wire fence. Again there is no path and again the walker has to scramble over heather, bearing towards the left and Low Beck. This cuts its way through a lovely gill, with yellowing larch on the far side and dark firs on the other.

The beck enters the forest in a series of charming waterfalls set against a golden backcloth as larch needles, bracken fronds, rowan and birch catch the late-afternoon sun. The beck leaps exuberantly down a deep fissure into a rock pool, sending spray in all directions. The beck falls again into another pool and then falls for a third time in a long column of water through a steep-sided gorge guarded by a red berried holly. This waterfall is a grand climax to a superb walk but do not tarry to admire it for too long

because the light goes quickly in the late afternoon of an early
November day. Cross the beck and the wire fence and follow a
forest path that drops straight down the fellside for several
hundred feet to the forest road. Turn left and follow the road until
it comes to the concrete bridge over the Liza. Unfortunately, the
walker still has to tackle the long uphill trek beside the lake to the
car.

Fly Agaric

O.S. Map NY134132 149132
10 miles.

Lodore Falls, Derwent Water

I n early December a westerly gale makes one seek a sheltered walk, such as a visit to the Lodore Falls. One can leave the car in the National Trust's Kettlewell car park with its bonnet facing the lake, so that one can picnic and perhaps watch a peregrine hurtling down on to a flock of mallard. Cross the road and take a signposted path which leads off to the right through Strutta Wood. Cross the beck by the log footbridge and pause beneath the near-vertical fall that drops through Lowcrag Wood. In summer its elegance is hidden in a silvan chasm but now the leafless trees are unable to hide its glory.

After enjoying this fall in Cat Gill (not to be confused with the Cat Gill falls below Walla Crag) continue along the footpath below Screes Coppice until it rejoins the road when it meets the boundary walls of the Lodore Hotel. Turn left here and follow a path, enticed onwards by the thunder of the Lodore. A red squirrel sits on a low branch of a holly tree devouring an acorn, unaware of the approach of the walker because of the noise of the waterfall. The woodland floor is deep in beech and oak

Long-tailed tit troop through the trees.

View of the lake through the trees

leaves and these scatter when a light breeze lifts them. Only in the tree tops is there evidence of a gale blowing.

In the nineteenth century Robert Southey wrote the poem, 'How does the water come down at Lodore?' In the twentieth, the Watendlath Beck makes its great descent in the same breath-taking way. Two huge bluffs of rock, Shepherds Crag and Gowder Crag, tower upwards, darkening all below, but the gloom is lightened by the foam-topped fall of water that descends impetuously, exuberantly and tumultuously for forty feet. Blue tit and long-tailed tit troop through the trees, their twittering lost in the noise of the roaring beck.

The oak, ash, larch and silver birch that clothe the precipitous sides are now leafless but here and there a holly grows with glossy, green leaves. An ancient birch is blanketed in moss which in turn supports young fern right up to the tree's crown. All the flat surfaces of rocks and boulders are covered in matted moss, spangled with tiny green leaves of bilberry. Climb up beside the water as it rages through narrow cuttings and crashes against enormous boulders. Sometimes it is brown but more often white with foam flecked with rust.

At times the going is easy. At others fallen trees and huge outcrops bar the path but these obstructions can be scrambled over without too much difficulty. Continue climbing carefully beside the angry, roaring Watendlath, whose tremendous volume of water fills the great cleft with fine spray. There is a dark whirlpool at the top of the falls as the water builds up before its leap. Stop here and

enjoy
the view
of Derwent
Water far
below. In
summer this
view is
obscured by the
dense foliage of the
trees but in December the
lake can be seen sparkling in
the thin winter sun.

Top of the falls

Now the path levels out and
walking becomes easier. Again the
noise of the beck allows one to come
upon another red squirrel feeding on
a nut. This is held tightly by its front
paws against its white vest. For a long
time it feeds and watches and feeds
again quite unperturbed by the
observer. Then it becomes aware of
the dog and bounds away up the steep
side of the gorge. Ahead lies a small
canyon and the path climbs up to the
left to avoid the sheer rock face. The beck cascades through the
narrow cutting with a pretty foaming, unlike its petulance lower
down.

After a short steep climb, join a reinforced path that runs
parallel with the beck. This circumvents the falls in the canyon.
Within a hundred yards, take a right turn on to a path that
returns to the side of the beck. Continue beside the hurrying
water, leaving the Crags behind, and enjoy the winter sunshine,
now no longer shut out by the steep rock walls. Follow the path
beside the beck on to a tiny promontory to view another waterfall.
Here jagged, spiked rocks point upwards through the raging water.
White foam piles up within the imprisoning sides and spray falls
on vegetation and viewer alike. Below, the racing, frothing water
snatches at the base of the little promontory and then thunders on
its way.

Retrace the path for a few steps, and cross a wall to the path on the other side. Here the beck is placid, and it flows in a wide arc around a small island on which grows a larch and an oak. The beck can be forded when the river is not in spate. Very soon the beckside path rejoins the reinforced path walked along earlier. Turn left and keep to the main path. As it descends it keeps the Watendlath within sight and sound but the beck's tantrums are hidden in the steep, sharp folds of the confining walls. Not so the lake, which reveals its charms for most of the walk downhill. At the bottom of the path look to the left to the white swathe of water — the Lodore Falls, still coming down as Southey wrote.

Kestrel hovering

O.S. Map NY265188
2 miles

Scale Force, Crummock Water, Buttermere

Scale Force, Crummock Water, Buttermere

From the village of Buttermere a bridlepath crosses the flat fields between Buttermere and Crummock Water. In late December the village is deserted except for the farmer taking fodder to his stock and sheep wandering through the narrow roads. A chill wind blows off Crummock Water and a mixed flock of chaffinch, wren, blackbird, brambling and goldcrest seek shelter in the thorn bushes lining the path. They keep out of the wind here and are quite unperturbed by passers-by. At this time of year the water in the beck between the two lakes is deep and dark as it flows under Scale Bridge. Reeds, not usually submerged, are pulled out by the current. In the willow along the banks a flock of long-tailed tit give a touch of colour to the greyness of the winter's day.

The path to the waterfalls is well signposted and leads off to the right. It passes through an ancient oak wood, now bare of leaves. Very soon it leaves the trees behind and comes near to Buttermere Dubs, where the wind blowing off the water and the current of the beck oppose each other, creating small eddies and

Scale Bridge

Geese on the shore line and brambling.

whirlpools. Here mallard pairs are busily concerned with each other. The well-worn path leads out to the fell and to a few wizened hawthorn which play host to a flock of excited fieldfare. These birds devour the berries in a careless, wanton way, scattering many on the ground, before they fly off to continue their feasting elsewhere.

Below to the right lies Crummock Water, and on one of the Holme Islands are several cormorant. One perches in an ungainly fashion on the top of a dead tree, its neck held like a question mark. A small flock of pochard dive frequently for weed growing in the shallows close to the islands. Beyond, a gaggle of black and white geese feed along the shore-line. The path then makes an abrupt left turn upwards, avoiding the very wet area ahead. A line of well-placed cairns guides the walker along a rocky track that requires much concentration to negotiate. The fellside is covered with dead bracken and bleached grass. All around, the sombre, handsome mountains tower upwards and there is a dusting of snow on their tops.

When a gap in a wall is reached the noise of falling water can be heard. A short clamber over red boulders and Scale Force is revealed. It drops in one continuous fall for over 100 ft, hurtling through a narrow cleft. Holly bushes clothe the sides of the cleft, maintaining a hold where any small ledge provides sufficient soil and nutrients. Some of the hollies are bright with berries and these are devoured in restless haste by more fieldfare. This very long fall of white water drops into a deep pool surrounded by rush. But still its descent is not finished because the water races on and divides into several traces that rage around a buttress of rock. One small side-fall drops delicately over red rock steps into a brown pool that is surrounded by heather still in bloom, lush green fern, carpets of liverwort, wood sorrel, saxifrage and foxglove.

Here, out of the wind, where frost and snow have not penetrated, is a different world from the lifeless fell — a tiny oasis of lush vegetation. It is good to sit at the foot of this dramatic fall and ponder awhile at the sheer magnificence of Scale Force.

View of Crummock Water from foot of waterfall.

O.S. Map NY151171
5 miles

Waterfalls on Comb Beck,
Buttermere

Waterfalls on Comb Beck, Buttermere

Buttermere: the name conjures up a picture of tranquil water, crags rising sharply, mixed woodland, charming lakeside paths, white-topped becks, tree creeper, tufted duck and a clear translucent light — a place to come to for mental refreshment at any time of the year. It is a good choice for a sunny December day at the year's end, but the walker should make an early start because the sun drops below the mountains by mid-day.

Park in Gatesgarth car park by Gatesgarthdale Beck at the foot of the road over the Honister Pass. Cross the road and follow the footpath through the farm where sheep are being dosed and geese cackle at passers-by. The path runs beside the ash-lined beck where mallard have now paired. Follow the path across the flat pasture land, with a group of fine pine away to the left. Cross the bridge and turn right beyond the next gate, walking along a path

Scots pine below Fleetwith Pike.

that keeps well above the lake. The latter is still, clear and sparkling in the bright sun. In the distance the waterfalls can be seen, white and angry.

At Comb Beck turn left and climb up beside the racing water. The rocks that cause the water to boil are covered with ice, and long icicles hang from crevices. Fifty yards or so up the fell a series of pretty cascades spread out fan-like under ash and birch. Another steep scramble brings one to the bottom of the waterfall. Comb Beck rises in Burtness Comb, below the serrated edges of Comb Crags. It cascades and falls through rough fell before leaping over a lip of rock in two white jets. Narrow ledges spread the water, and it becomes a lace-like curtain of white foam. The confining rock-faces are casketed in ice. More long icicles hang and sparkle. Lattices of ice cover flat surfaces all the way down the beck and around the blue pool into which it plummets. A single larch guards this long fall.

The beck races through the pool and is divided into several streams where gigantic boulders lie athwart the water. Below this the beck swirls around a grassy island supporting one splendid rowan. With care, return down the icy fell over grass thick with frost and where every formerly wet patch is now frozen hard. After crossing the bridge over the beck, walk along the path under larch to a gate into Burtness Wood. Here the over-mature larch are being felled and replaced with oak. Some larch are being left for screening.

When the path divides take the shore path and enjoy the reflections in the sunlit water. Across the lake is Whiteless Pike, and behind it Grasmoor is covered with snow. Towards the end of the lake all other sounds are blotted out by the tremendous fall of water descending Sourmilk Gill, visited in August. Stand on the bridge and look at this magnificent waterfall and the lush vegetation clothing its steep sides. Turn right here, crossing the two bridges and passing beneath some oak. These are covered with a dense mat of moss, and a pair of tree creeper, unworried by visitors, are busily dispatching luckless insects. The path lies over a field and through a gate that eventually leads to the side of the Fish Hotel in the village of Buttermere. In the hedgerows bordering the path are chaffinch, blue and great tit, blackbird, house and hedge sparrow and several robin.

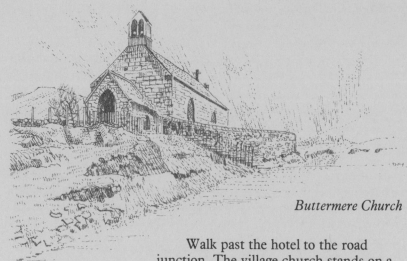

Buttermere Church

Walk past the hotel to the road junction. The village church stands on a small hill. Turn right where a signpost directs to the shore path. Pass through a farm, then through another gate and turn right at the next signpost. Scramble over a huge rock and take the path along the shore. Here the edges of the lake are frozen and the ice glistens in the last of the sun. Tufted duck dive quickly a little way from the shore. The path has several kissing gates and runs beneath silver birch and oak. All is utterly quiet except for the sound of falling water in Sourmilk Gill on the other side of the lake. Red Pike, above the gill, comes into view, and the rocks, giving the mountain its name, glow a rich red in the sun. Soon Comb Beck waterfall can be seen across the lake and its whole length is reflected in the still water, a magical sight.

Farther along, the path is edged with fine beech, lime, sycamore, ash and oak.

Tunnel hewn many years ago.

Ahead lies the entrance to a short tunnel, hewn many years ago when the landowner of the area decided that his workforce should not idle away the wet days. The tunnel is nearly six feet high and 30 feet long and is rather damp. It is just long enough for one to imagine the hewers and their conversation, and to realise how hard their work must have been. Continue along the lake shore until the path reaches the road. Even here a track runs beside the tarmac. But for the final eighth-of-a-mile to the car park one must walk along the road itself.

This excellent walk takes one past two superb waterfalls. It is so well arranged that it is impossible to get lost or to stray on to private land. An ideal way to end the year.

Hazel Nuts

O.S. Map NY183152
5 miles